M000224131

The
LAKE ERIE
CAMPAIGN
of 1813

I Shall Fight Them This Day

WALTER P. RYBKA

THE
History
PRESS

Published by The History Press
Charleston, SC 29403
www.historypress.net

Front cover image: This representation of the battle on Lake Erie is respectfully inscribed to Commodore Perry, his officers and gallant crews, by their humble servant James Webster (1815). A contemporary nineteenth-century rendition, this painting captures the dramatic nature of the battle and shows details such as the damage to the *Lawrence* and Perry's transfer by boat to the *Niagara*. Few naval battle scenes were painted by eyewitnesses or seamen and are inherently conjectural. *Courtesy Library of Congress.*

Drawings, diagrams and simplified maps are from author's drawings, enhanced by fonts and sorted appropriate line weights by computer graphic artist Damon Klep.

First published 2012
Second printing 2013

ISBN 978.1.54020.735.7

Library of Congress CIP data applied for.

CONTENTS

PRELUDE TO BATTLE

Western end of Lake Erie, September 10, 1813, late morning.

Under a hot sun in a clear sky, a light southeast breeze barely ruffles the surface of Lake Erie. On that tranquil blue-green surface, fifteen sailing ships glide at a walking pace in two lines, slowly converging. Six of them fly the Union Jack on White Ensign of the Royal Navy, while nine sail under the Stars and Stripes. On board each vessel, the only sounds are the faint ripple of water at the bows and the tense breathing of men acutely aware that they are "standing into danger." All possible preparations having been completed hours ago, the men have nothing to do but stand silent at their stations, contemplating their fate with emotions that can only be fully understood by those who have seen battle. Outwardly calm, showing a grim resolve to do their duty and to not let their shipmates down, each confront a fear of mutilation, death and, perhaps most of all, being found wanting in the trial ahead. As the minutes drag by, the opposing lines draw closer, "in that dread silence that precedes a hurricane."

As the heat of the sun increases on the back of his blue woolen jacket, perhaps Oliver Hazard Perry thinks for a moment of the day nearly seven months earlier when he arrived at Erie in a bone-chilling cold that no amount of wool could keep out. All the months of toil since have led up to this moment. Actually, all of the sixteen years since first joining the navy have been preparing Perry for what he confides "is the most important day of my life."

It is nearing noon, and white sails draw silently across a blue sky. Fresh paint glistens on the hulls and reflects off the waters. Suddenly, music wafts over the lake. On board the **HMS** *Detroit*, the band has struck up "Rule Britannia!" As the tune wanes, a puff of flame and smoke is followed by the crash of a twenty-four-pounder firing, the discharge of powder followed for several seconds by the distinctive tearing sound of the ball boring through the air. A splash and a plume of spray mark the fall, short of the American ships. In less than three minutes, the heavy gun has been reloaded, and the British gun captain has skillfully made a slight adjustment to the elevation. Again the spout of flame and smoke is seen by the Americans a moment before the sound travels over the still water. Again the sound of round shot tearing air, this time followed by the loud *thwock* of the ball striking the bulwark planking of the *Lawrence*. The crash of splintered timber brings with it a short shriek, as the first man dies in the Battle of Lake Erie.

A few months earlier, that man and most of his American shipmates had never heard of Lake Erie. Or if they had, it was only in the context of a wilderness outpost offering backbreaking work, uncharted rock-strewn waters, poor food and the danger of Indian attack. Yet they volunteered. What brought these men to this moment of supreme challenge?

PREFACE

It has been my great privilege to have served as master, or by courtesy "Captain," of the current U.S. brig *Niagara* since 1991, and many are the times that I have envisioned the previous scenario while sailing over the actual battle site in the western part of Lake Erie. Ship's decks have served as stages for many of history's most intense dramas, and the Battle of Lake Erie surely qualifies as one of them. In a story so often told, my sole claim on the reader's attention is my view of these events through the lens of a seaman's eye. It is my hope to impart just enough knowledge of the operational capabilities and constraints of wooden sailing ships in this environment that the reader might gain a better appreciation of the difficulties faced and the options open to the original participants. In this abridged version, the author's illustrations must carry the primary load in conveying the technical side of the story, which is needed to fully understand the courage shown and evaluate the choices made by those who sailed and fought here in 1813.

This book started out with the intention of offering the definitive text on the Battle of Lake Erie, including comparison of differing accounts and in-depth sourcing. Although the inputs and insights for the narrative grew out of two decades of work with the present brig *Niagara* and the Erie Maritime Museum, the writing of it has been entirely a private project squeezed into the early hours of the morning or the last minutes of the day. As the manuscript grew, I requested review from several professional historians and professors, who generously waded through it and gave me much sound advice (however much they contradicted one another). Publishers were understandably leery of a large work by a first-time author. Combine all of these factors, and the idea of getting a book out for the bicentennial of the War of 1812 was becoming an ever-receding mirage.

What rescued the effort was a request from Dr. William Garvey, himself a professor of history, retired president of Mercyhurst College and founding president of the Jefferson Education Society, Erie's think tank. The Jefferson created a subgroup, the Perry 200, for the purpose of making educational events happen for the bicentennial of the War of 1812. Dr. Garvey told me that what was needed for the occasion was a short book, affordable and accessible, to give the average citizen a context for the historic events that originated in Erie and a concise account of the naval campaign. His encouragement, and that of the Perry 200 publications committee, was the reason this book is seeing the light of day.

I also wish to acknowledge the unstinting generosity of Gerard T. Altoff, who over many years as the National Park Service historian at Perry's Victory National Monument shared much of his knowledge and steered me toward much more. Further thanks go to Linda Bolla, volunteer educator at the Erie Maritime Museum, whose assistance in tracking down illustrations was invaluable. Also, my thanks to Penny and Elizabeth, my wife and daughter, for their support and patience through this effort.

SOURCES

As an overview to brief a reader on the war and place the Lake Erie Campaign in context, the first chapter relies heavily on secondary sources. Several authors produced books under the same title (*The War of 1812*): Donald Hickey best combines the political decision-making with the military story; John K. Mahon emphasizes battles; Reginald Horsman is strong on logistical factors; Henry James is heavy on political factors; and Donald Graves gives the Canadian point of view. Pierre Berton's *Invasion of Canada and Flames Across the Border* relates personal Canadian stories, as does Alan Taylor's *The Civil War of 1812*.

For naval affairs, *The Naval War of 1812* by Theodore Roosevelt remains sound, as does *Seapower in Its Relations to the War of 1812* by Alfred Thayer Mahan. *The Naval War of 1812: A Documentary History* (vols. 1–2 edited by William S. Dudley, and vol. 3 edited by Michael J. Crawford), from the Naval Historical Center, gives in-depth access to original sources in their own words. For the Lake Erie Campaign, the standard work remains *Signal Victory* by

David Curtis Skaggs and Gerard T. Altoff. In addition, the collected works of Altoff, written over many years as National Park Service historian at Perry's Victory and International Peace Monument, are highly recommended, as is Rosenberg's *The Building of Perry's Fleet*. Emily McCain's study *Ghost Ships, Hamilton and Scourge: Historical Treasures from the War of 1812* and Thomas and Robert Malcomson's *HMS Detroit: The Battle for Lake Erie* are essential reading as well. Dozens more were consulted, as well as unpublished archival sources, but those listed here are most accessible to the general reader.

The rest of the book relies primarily on transcripts of unpublished archival material assembled by the Pennsylvania Historical and Museum Commission (PHMC) to guide and inform the interpretation of the U.S. brig *Niagara* and the Erie Maritime Museum. The Perry Papers (fourteen boxes) belong to the William L. Clements Library at the University of Michigan in Ann Arbor. Transcription of letters relevant to the Lake Erie Campaign was the work of Gerard T. Altoff.

The records of the Department of the Navy, now in the Naval Historical Center, Washington D.C., are in several collections, such as letters to officers, generally from the secretary of the navy to ship commanders, with the replies gathered in the letter books of Isaac Chauncey, O.H. Perry and so forth. These, too, were transcribed by G.T. Altoff. Many of these letters are also found in the documentary history assembled by W.S. Dudley. The Naval Historical Center also holds transcripts of Royal Navy commander R.H. Barclay's court-martial proceedings and his after-action report to his superior, Sir James Yeo, originals of which are in the PRO London, United Kingdom. The diary of Samuel Hambleton, squadron purser and personal friend of O.H. Perry, is an unpublished manuscript held by the Maryland Historical Society in Baltimore, transcription by G.T. Altoff.

Much of the writings of Surgeon Usher Parsons, including his casualty report from the Battle of Lake Erie, are held by the Rhode Island Historical Society in Providence, Rhode Island. The journal of the *Lawrence*, by Sailing Master W.V. Taylor, is the only known surviving logbook of the Lake Erie squadron and is held with other Taylor letters and affidavits by the Newport Historical Society, Newport, Rhode Island. Transcription of these documents was the work of the late PHMC historian Robert Eaton. All of these transcripts are available to researchers at the Erie Maritime Museum, Erie Pennsylvania. Also, the Daniel Dobbins Papers are held by the Erie County Historical Society in Buffalo, New York, with microfilm copies available at the Erie County Historical Society in Erie, Pennsylvania. The originals in Buffalo, New York, were examined by this author.

The original manuscript was prepared with conventional endnotes and citations required for an academic work. The purpose of this book, condensed and compacted, is to offer an affordable guide aimed at the general reader wondering what the bicentennial of the War of 1812 is about. As such, it required choosing between deleting individual source notes (from this edition) and leaving out at least one-third of the narrative. It is my hope that by offering more of a narrative, readers new to the story may find the subject of interest enough to seek more information later. In places where particularly important quotes are used, or where crucial interpretation relies on unpublished sources, a mention of such sources is made in the text.

AN OVERVIEW OF THE
WAR OF 1812

CAUSES

A mericans often refer to the War of 1812 as the "Second War of Independence." In much of the American literature, the war is seen as a necessary end to British domination over North America. This is an overstatement. America's existence as a nation was not at stake, but freedom of trade and economic growth certainly were. The United States declared war on Great Britain in response to British policies that violated American rights. These policies, however highhanded and oppressive, were the result of Britain's struggle for survival against revolutionary France. Although French and British policies were nearly identical regarding restricting the other's trade, the great superiority of Britain's Royal Navy (RN) kept most French ships in port and customarily defeated those that came out to fight. Consequently, many more American ships were seized by British warships than by French. The former colonists accordingly saw British oppression more clearly than French and saw themselves as resisting British tyranny just as they had a generation earlier during their Revolution.

Nowhere was this tyranny more evident than in the Royal Navy's practice of impressments. The Royal Navy preferred to be an all-volunteer service. When faced with wartime shortages, however, British law allowed for the impressment (equivalent to conscription) of seamen to meet the nation's needs. Under the strain of the French Revolutionary and Napoleonic Wars, the need was both severe and unending. Impressment had a ruthless logic. A

Naval warfare in the French Revolutionary and Napoleonic Wars. Depicted here is *The Battle of the First of June 1794* by Phillippe-Jacques de Loutherbourg (1795). The customary opponents, Great Britain's Royal Navy versus the French navy, the customary British victory and the customary "butcher's bill." *Courtesy of the National Maritime Museum.*

strong navy was absolutely necessary, merchant seamen were already trained as sailors and their vocation owed a special debt to the navy that kept pirates at bay and the sea lanes open to trade. Therefore, when the navy called, these men were expected to accept their lot. They generally did, despite the mind-boggling and needless cruelty of a system that suddenly took men away without warning and with only the clothes in which they stood.

Supposedly free men literally disappeared from the streets of their own communities, with no chance to provide for, bid farewell or even give notice to the wives, children and parents they might never see again. It is utterly astounding that men subjected to such emotional trauma—then, once on board a warship, treated like ill-used slaves—would later be lustily singing "Rule Britannia...Britons never never shall be slaves!" The naval command system was successful in convincing them that life would be worse under the French and that the quickest way home was victory over the French. That the seafaring life of the era was full of danger and hardship, even in peacetime, lent a certain fatalism to their attitude. At least in most of the wars of the eighteenth century, naval commissions were of limited duration, and the men had a fair prospect of being released in three or four years.

The war that began in 1792, however, saw only a brief truce between 1801 and 1803 and then resumed until 1814. The Royal Navy was chronically short of men but could afford no lessening of force. The harsh discipline and low pay were bad enough, but faced with interminable service, men deserted in ever-higher numbers when opportunity afforded. Fear of desertion caused commanding officers to deny shore leave. Naturally, the indefinite isolation from friends and family from denial of leave created more pressure to desert. The Royal Navy had stumbled into a vicious cycle that exacerbated the problem. The best opportunity to desert would be in a U.S. port, where Royal Navy vessels frequently put in to purchase provisions. Alternatively, a deserter might seek to join the crew of an American merchant ship in some neutral port. The U.S. merchant marine was doing a booming trade and paid good wages in a labor-short market plus there was no language barrier.

Confronted with significant manpower losses, the Royal Navy resorted to stopping merchant ships of all nations to search for British deserters, as well as contraband cargo. At the time, there was no international law against searching merchant vessels at sea, let alone when near British home waters. The American doctrine that the flag protected the ship as an extension of the nation was unique at the time. To add insult to injury, British warships put in to U.S. ports to reprovision and then sometimes remained near the approaches to intercept ships as if blockading a hostile port. Searches in British home waters were to be expected, but Americans found it particularly infuriating to have their ships stopped and searched in U.S. coastal waters immediately upon departure. It was one thing to accept the risks of venturing into a European war zone. But the chance of being impressed from a ship on a domestic voyage along the U.S. coast was another level of threat that meant no one was safe.

When searched, the practical difficulty became identifying British nationals. There were no fingerprints, photos or passports, and there was less difference in accent or manner than at present. In an attempt to provide identification, U.S. Customs officers were authorized to issue Seaman's Protection Certificates attesting to the American citizenship of an individual based on parish registers, birth records in a family bible or sworn testimony from the applicant and a witness. Royal Navy officers generally disregarded such certificates because forgeries were readily for sale in waterfront taverns. Seamen from a common stock and sharing a common language blended

Impressment scene. Constantly short of men, and desperately seeking to stem the flow of deserters, British warships searched the merchant ships of all nations seeking British nationals for compulsory naval service. Without reliable means of identification, thousands of Americans were swept up in this cruel system during the decade leading up to the War of 1812. *Impressment of American Seaman*, from a drawing by Howard Pyle. *Courtesy Library of Congress.*

easily, and neither legal interpretation nor physical identity offered certainty of nationality.

To Americans, these former British seamen were immigrants seeking new lives. To the Royal Navy, they were subjects of the Crown and liable for military service. The British claimed no right to impress other than their own citizens, and they did, in fact, release Americans when adequate proof of U.S. birth could be produced. Such proof consisted of affidavits and letters from sufficiently high-ranking U.S. officials to show that the case was taken seriously. Inevitably, this process took months if not years, with the unfortunate impressed seaman subject to the rigors and dangers of forced service during the interval. Estimates suggest that from six thousand to ten thousand Americans were impressed in the decade before 1812. Impressment became a worse problem each year after 1803. Despite the hazards, American merchants were doing very well out of the European war, until the Berlin Decree and the Orders in Council threatened to destroy European trade. The United States' drift toward war began in 1807.

American sentiment against Britain was strong, but internal dissent centered on the feasibility of fighting. Those who were for investing in a strong navy and army were countered by those who feared higher taxation and large military establishments more than they feared the British. From 1807 to 1809, the Jefferson administration tried unilateral trade sanctions—nonimportation acts and an embargo on exports intended to force both Britain and France to rescind their restrictive decrees. This policy proved a catastrophic failure. The fatal flaw of the embargo lay in grossly overestimating the importance of U.S. goods to the European economy. In truth, it was the other way around.

The truly astounding fact is the extent to which the law was obeyed, at least for the first few months. As revenue plummeted, unemployment rose and with it contempt for the law in the form of smuggling. After nearly two years, the acts were rescinded, but not before many merchants and shipbuilders had been bankrupted. Equally unfathomable, the federal government had elected to starve itself. In this era, customs duties were the largest source of government revenue, and these measures cut them off. All that had been accomplished was to highlight American weakness. The country had seriously damaged both its economy and self-confidence through the self-inflicted wound of an unrealistic policy.

The drift toward war was slow and reluctant, but by the winter of 1811–12, it had acquired a momentum built of cumulative despair. Economic hardship, the open wound of impressment and injured pride were convincing more Americans to seek redress through war. The president sent a war message to Congress on June 1, 1812, but debate and expectation had been building for months. The expectation of war was such that another embargo was enacted in April, calculated to allow ships already in Europe enough time to get home while preventing outbound vessels from getting caught in a British port.

After much debate, the U.S. Congress declared war on Great Britain on June 18, 1812, from a political position of spectacular weakness, with 40 percent of votes in the House and Senate dissenting. It was a tragic irony that while Americans were declaring war, the British ministers were rethinking the problem, largely due to their own merchants' bitter complaints of lost revenue from the restrictions on American trade. The British blockade policy was rescinded on June 23, five days after the declaration of war. Since news could only travel by sailing ship, the British learned of the American declaration of war on July 29, while news of the rescinded blockade reached Washington on August 12, 1812.

As much as American anger had been building, considering the closeness of the vote for war, it is very likely that had the Orders in Council been rescinded a few weeks earlier, there would have been no war. Impressment would have remained an unresolved issue, but by itself it would have been unlikely to bring on a war. The extent of the war vote dissent didn't arise from sympathy for Britain but rather from an appreciation of how difficult it would be to fight the world's most powerful navy and one of the strongest armies—the nation was about to find out just how difficult. American hopes for a quick settlement with Great Britain were pinned to expectations of Napoleon's continued success. More bad timing. Just as the United States declared war on Great Britain, Napoleon set out for Moscow with more than 400,000 men though fewer than 10,000 came back. British success in driving the French out of Spain, coupled with the French catastrophe in Russia, did not augur well for U.S. hopes. It is another irony of this war that the United States entered it filled with righteous conviction that we were preserving freedom, while relying on the further success of a ruthless dictator, Napoleon, to keep British forces occupied so that we could do so.

STRATEGIC COMPARISONS

The primary war aims of the United States were to force Britain to rescind trade sanctions and to end the impressment of seamen from American ships. A secondary aim was to halt British support for Native American resistance to U.S. westward expansion. Implicit in all three was the defense of national honor against overbearing British influence. Before the war, some Americans openly advocated the conquest of Canada, but this was not a majority view. Nevertheless, invading Canada appeared the best means of putting pressure on Britain. Once war was declared, conquest of Canada became a primary military objective. Disruption of British trade through capture of merchant shipping was an equally obvious way to inflict economic hardship. Both by land and by sea, the best defense was deemed to be a good offense.

The means to carry out these intentions were ludicrously inadequate. While tensions had been building for years, no effective preparations had been made. The U.S. Navy (USN) had 16 combatant ships (7 frigates, 9 sloops of war) and a few lesser vessels. The Royal Navy had a strength of 740 ships (nearly 100 ships of the line, more than 200 frigates and many sloops of war and auxiliaries). Even with Britain's worldwide commitments, their North American squadron alone had 25 vessels (1 ship of the line, 7 frigates, 7 sloops, 7 brigs and 3 schooners). This single backwater squadron was considerably stronger than the entire U.S. Navy.

The disparity of personnel between the two navies was also prominent: USN, all ranks, about 6,000, versus Royal Navy, all ranks, about 145,000, or nearly 24:1. The U.S. Army had an authorized strength of more than 35,000, but only about 7,000 were actually in service, with mostly low levels of training, poor equipment and troops nearly devoid of combat experience. Most of these men were stationed on the western frontier to defend against Indian attacks. The British army of 229,000 regulars had been tested in fierce combat in Europe for most of the preceding two decades. The 8,000 British troops in Canada alone were more than a match for the entire U.S. Army. Yet it was the Americans who declared war. What were they thinking?

The civilian leadership of the United States had a profound distrust of a professional military, fearing both its cost and its potential for political interference. Instead they cherished the ideal of the local militia—citizen soldiers called up for brief terms in the national defense. Likewise at sea, the navy would be supplemented by privateers, privately owned vessels licensed by the federal government to prey on the shipping of an enemy nation. The militia proved of little use in the actual war, and privateers sailed to seize wealth, not fight for strategic objectives. Short-term amateurs are rarely a match for professionals in any line of work, let alone in the serious and deadly business of warfare. Very few of America's political leaders had any military experience, not even as observers of the European wars. There were then no equivalents to the Central Intelligence Agency, Office of Naval Intelligence, National Security Agency or Jane's Fighting Ships. In today's parlance, the U.S. situation would be described as a catastrophic "intelligence failure." In short, the nation had only the vaguest idea of what it was up against.

The Opening Campaign

It was not long in finding out. As could have been expected, the war began badly for the United States. It has become a cliché that U.S. leaders shared President Thomas Jefferson's belief that "the conquest of Canada is a mere matter of marching." With a little serious preparation, it might have been. The British had few troops stationed in Canada and thought Upper Canada (Ontario), at least, to be all but indefensible. The Americans intended a three-pronged offensive at the Detroit River, across the Niagara River and along the Hudson-Richelieu River corridor toward Montreal.

By accident, British forces in Canada learned of the declaration of war before the Americans in the northwest. International businessman and fur trader John Jacob Astor was in Washington when war was declared. Instantly recognizing a threat to his business, he sent dispatch riders galloping to the border to inform his agents to halt all fur shipments lest they be seized. This action, taken for purely personal business reasons, had the side effect of spreading the news like wildfire on the Canadian side of the border. Small forces of redcoats, with larger groups of Indian allies, quickly surprised and captured the tiny garrisons at Fort Dearborn (Chicago) and Fort Mackinac. The first U.S. offensive action came in July when Brigadier General William Hull led a few hundred troops across the Detroit River to attack Fort Malden, but the attack never took place. Upon learning that Fort Mackinac had fallen, that Indians were astride his supply routes and that British reinforcements were on the way, Hull retreated to Detroit.

Under the command of Major General Sir Isaac Brock, British forces in Upper Canada then seized the initiative. Brock used the vessels of the Provincial Marine, a Canadian government transport service, and a fleet of bateaux to rapidly shift his men toward Detroit from the Niagara Peninsula. Though Brock had only half the number of Hull's soldiers and much less artillery, he did have several thousand Indian allies who were gathered together by the great Shawnee chief Tecumseh. Brock coolly bluffed Hull into the bloodless surrender of Detroit along with 2,500 men and all weapons and stores by hinting at the possibility of not being able to restrain his Indian allies from massacring both the garrison and townspeople if the fort fell.

As a result of Hull's surrender, the entire Michigan territory fell, and it quickly became the Americans who feared invasion. Brock next shifted the bulk of his force back to the east in defense of the Niagara Peninsula. In October, American forces attempted an invasion across the Niagara River, and the Battle of Queenstown Heights proved another disaster for the United States. With the majority of the assault force killed or captured, no further attempt could be made that year. General Brock's death at Queenstown Heights was a setback for the British and granted some respite to the U.S. forces to recover unmolested from their blunders.

The year's final U.S. fiasco came in November when a poorly organized expedition advanced to take Cole Mill, just over the New York–Canadian border north of Lake Champlain. Unbeknownst to the Americans, the Canadians had abandoned the place as indefensible. However, in a dense fog, U.S. forces advancing in two columns encountered each other, with tragic results. The demoralized Americans withdrew, and troops on both sides of the border went into winter quarters. As the winter of 1812–13 set in, the entire U.S. northern frontier seemed in peril. The consequences for the United

States were not worse solely because American incompetence was matched by British weakness, which restricted them to a defensive strategy in Canada.

THE WAR AT SEA

In complete contrast to the repeated defeats on land, Americans proudly remember the opening months of the war at sea for a string of U.S. victories in single-ship actions including *Constitution* versus *Guerriere*, *Wasp* versus *Frolic*, *United States* versus *Macedonian*, *Constitution* versus *Java*, *Hornet* versus *Peacock* and *Essex* versus *Alert*. The U.S. policy of building maximum fighting power into the few ships it had proved effective. In each of these contests, the U.S. vessel significantly outgunned its opponent by virtue of the American practice of building frigates larger and heavier—and thus able to carry a heavier armament—than equivalent classes in any other navy. These victories produced a euphoria in the United States.

In the years leading up to the war, the Royal Navy had been the instrument for impressment of seamen and the seizure of ships that had led to the war. Furthermore, in the preceding decades of the Anglo-French war, the British had fought hundreds of ship-to-ship actions, as well as numerous large fleet actions. The Royal Navy had won all of the fleet actions and all but a few of the ship-to-ship duels. So great was the Royal Navy's reputation that in the Congressional debates over war measures, one of the arguments against building a larger U.S. Navy was that whatever the United States built the British were sure to capture or destroy. But celebrations in the United States were short-lived. The British responded quickly by simply reallocating a little more of their overall strength to the North American station. By mid-1813, most U.S. ships, both naval and merchant, had been blockaded in their own ports.

Fast-sailing privateers frequently eluded the blockade and made it to sea throughout the war. Privateers have a special niche in the American imagination, combining the daring of a David v. Goliath story for patriotic purposes with independent free enterprise rewarded by great wealth. Like most get-rich-quick schemes, however, the reality fell short of the promise. Very few grew very wealthy, while many more went broke. At least one-third were captured by the Royal Navy, and roughly half of the prizes taken were subsequently recaptured. U.S. privateers drove up British insurance rates and thus became a thorn in the side of the British. These same privateers were also a thorn in the side of the U.S. Navy since they were in direct competition for recruitment of seamen.

USS *Constitution* defeats HMS *Guerriere*, August 19, 1812. In the opening months of the war, the USN surprised the RN, and just about everybody else, with a series of victories in single-ship actions. The U.S. practice of building maximum fighting power into the few ships it had was a success. While good for American morale, these victories had no measurable impact on the strategic balance, in which weight of numbers gave Britain the upper hand at sea for the duration. *Action between USS Constitution and HMS Guerriere, 19 August 1812*, by Michel Felice Corne. *Courtesy Naval History & Heritage Command Photographic Department.*

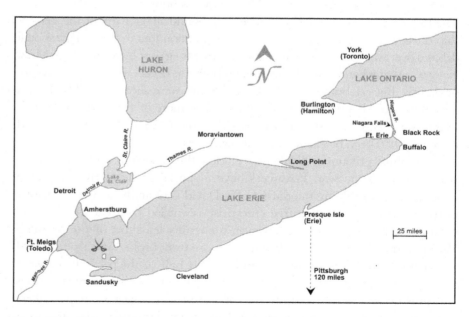

Map of Lake Erie and adjacent area. In a largely roadless wilderness, control of the waterways was the key strategic objective for both sides.

For the rest of the war, U.S. warships ships got through the British blockades only sporadically, and a few individual ship duels occurred each year. The numbers of vessels lost by both sides were nearly equal, while the only fleet actions took place on the northern Lakes. Of these, several were fought on Lake Ontario, but all ended in draws. Only two decisive fleet actions were fought during the war, the Lake Erie and Lake Champlain battles, both of which were U.S. victories.

STRATEGIC STALEMATE IN 1813

Back on land, the year 1813 began with more bad news. In January, a U.S. force attempting to recapture Detroit was all but wiped out at the River Raisin (Monroe, Michigan). As a direct result, the secretary of war ordered General William Henry Harrison, U.S. army commander in the northwest, to build up his forces but not attempt further advances until the U.S. Navy secured Lake Erie. It was this decision that drove the building of the Lake Erie squadron. The initial advantage in this struggle lay with the British, having had a few armed vessels on the Great Lakes before the war. These, however, were too weakly manned to take offensive action.

In the fall of 1812, the United States began building gunboats in Erie, Pennsylvania, and refitting and arming merchant ships at Black Rock, New York. The major U.S. shipbuilding effort was at Sackets Harbor, New York, on the eastern end of Lake Ontario, under the command of Captain Isaac Chauncey, formerly commandant of the New York naval station. Meanwhile, the British established Kingston, Ontario, as their principal base, commanded by Captain Sir James Lucas Yeo. Lesser building yards were at York (Toronto) and Amherstburg (on the Detroit River).

The strategic key to the entire region was the British east–west supply line along the St. Lawrence River. If passage of the river could be blocked, everything to the west would fall like a tree limb severed from its trunk. A U.S. attack on Quebec was never seriously considered since it was too heavily defended, too far from U.S. bases and too easily reinforced from England. Montreal, the obvious second choice, was also too well defended to be taken by the feeble U.S. forces. Taking Kingston, westernmost city on the St. Lawrence, became the next-best choice. Capturing it, however, required naval superiority on Lake Ontario. For this reason, both sides concentrated their major naval efforts at the eastern end of Lake Ontario throughout the war.

In April 1813, the Americans were not strong enough to attempt Kingston. Instead, U.S. Navy captain Isaac Chauncey made an amphibious assault on York (Toronto) on April 27, with great success. A partially built frigate was burned, as well as the fort and public buildings, but the cost was high. Just as the Americans reached the abandoned and burning fort, the magazine exploded, hurling a rain of stone on the advancing men. General Zebulon Pike, a rising star in the U.S. Army, was mortally wounded, as were nearly three hundred others. Still, the raid had a major impact. All military stores were either captured or destroyed, including the armament and other equipment intended for the British Lake Erie squadron. The seeds of British defeat on Lake Erie were sown this day. From Chauncey's report to Secretary of the Navy Jones:

> *The loss of stores at this place will be an irreparable one to the enemy, for independent of the difficulty of transportation, the articles cannot be replaced in this country. The provisions and clothing also taken and destroyed will be a serious loss to him. In fact, I believe, that he has recd. a blow that he cannot recover.*

A month later, Chauncey again sailed west, to the mouth of the Niagara River, transporting troops and providing shore bombardment support for a renewed invasion of Canada. The landing, on May 27, was initially a success. The British were compelled to abandon Forts George and Erie, retreating toward Burlington (Hamilton, Ontario). If the Americans had been able to hold Burlington, the British supply line to Lake Erie would have been severed. Instead, the British rallied, and on June 5, the Battle of Stony Creek, just east of Burlington, became the high-water mark of the American advance. Defeated, the Americans fell back on Fort George. In August and September, the large naval squadrons of Chauncey and Yeo engaged twice on Lake Ontario, but cautious maneuvering and long-range firing proved indecisive. Both commanders recognized that the loss of their squadrons would be an irremediable catastrophe that would likely lose the war for their side. Both chose caution over audacity, and a stalemate ensued on both Lake Ontario and the Niagara Peninsula for the rest of 1813.

At the western end of the Canadian/American frontier, British superiority was also being tested. In May, British general Henry Procter used the naval squadron at Amherstburg to carry troops and artillery to the Maumee River and lay siege to Fort Meigs, Ohio (just south of present-day Toledo). If Fort Meigs could be taken, not only would the Americans be pushed back farther from Detroit, but the Indians would also be greatly encouraged to remain

The burning of York (Toronto), April 1813. The United States made a successful raid, capturing the guns intended for the British Lake Erie squadron and for ships on the stocks for Lake Ontario. This burning and others invited reprisals later in the war, of which Washington is best remembered. *The Death of General Pike, at York, on the 27th of April, 1813,* National Archives of Canada.

British allies and perhaps launch raids into Ohio. Fort Meigs endured bombardment for five days behind its thick earthworks, with few casualties. A relief force of Kentuckians, however, marched into an Indian ambush south of the fort. Only 400 of 1,200 survived to reach the fort. After this bloody field success, the Indians would not stay for a siege, and the British artillery had run low on ammunition. Both factors prompted withdrawal.

Both sides claimed victory, the Americans for holding the fort, the British for having inflicted much higher casualties. Strategically, it was as much a failure for the British as the invasion of the Niagara Peninsula had been for the Americans. During August, British-Indian forces made a second attempt on Fort Meigs and also attacked Fort Stephenson, near Sandusky. Both attacks failed, and the British suffered heavy casualties. Serious enough in themselves, these losses also discredited the British to the Indians, whose intertribal alliance was falling apart. The tide of war was turning in the west.

Throughout the first half of 1813, an American squadron of six vessels was under construction at Erie, Pennsylvania. The American invasion of the Niagara Peninsula in May captured Fort Erie, whose guns had prevented five small merchant vessels undergoing conversion to gunboats at Black Rock from leaving the naval station. In June, Master Commandant Oliver H. Perry, the U.S. naval commander on Lake Erie, was able to move these vessels two miles upstream, out of the confines of the river and into Lake Erie.

While the American squadron was built under difficult circumstances, the chief problem facing the navy was lack of men to man the ships. Perry was only able to get the gunboats to Erie because his fifty-five officers and sailors were supplemented by two hundred infantry temporarily assigned to Perry. The British were dogged by the same problem to a far worse degree on their side of the lake. In August, Perry was finally ready to take to the lake. Faced with a much stronger squadron, the British fell back to their base at Amherstburg to await completion of a new and larger ship, the *Detroit*. For the next month, the Americans blockaded the Detroit River, and the British supply situation steadily deteriorated.

On September 10, 1813, the British squadron came out, more in desperation than in confidence, and met the Americans in the Battle of Lake Erie. After a hard-fought battle of more than three hours, the entire British squadron surrendered. The Americans had complete naval superiority on Lake Erie and used that advantage two weeks later to transport a portion of Harrison's army for an invasion of Canada. The British evacuated Amherstburg without a fight and fled east up the Thames River. Harrison's pursuit overtook and routed them at Moraviantown on October 5. Tecumseh, famous Shawnee chief and architect of the British-Indian alliance, died in this battle. Upon his death, the already weakening cohesion of the tribal alliances fell apart, removing a major threat to continued U.S. westward expansion.

The British collapse along the Detroit River left their right flank exposed all the way to the Niagara Peninsula. The American advance was spent, however, with militia enlistments soon to expire, supplies running low and winter not far off. Also, Harrison could not be sure of the level of hostility of the Indians still in his rear, and he thought it best to fall back to Detroit and consolidate the gains. Meanwhile on the Niagara Peninsula, as winter approached in December 1813, the British gathered enough strength to compel the Americans to abandon Forts George and Erie. In a move both cruel and stupid, the U.S. commander, thinking to deny winter quarters to the advancing British, burned the adjacent town of Newark to the ground.

The residents had a thirty-minute notice before being turned out into a snowstorm. Then the Americans panicked and retreated in such haste that they failed to burn Fort George. An aroused British force pursued them across the Niagara River and burned Buffalo and Black Rock in retaliation. Soon afterward, the British captured Fort Niagara, on the U.S. side of the river, in a surprise night attack and held it for the duration of the war.

At the eastern end of Lake Ontario, the Americans aimed another two-pronged attack at Montreal. In November, the force descending the St. Lawrence on the Canadian side was overtaken by British troops following from Kingston. The Battle of Chrysler's Farm was a sharp defeat for the Americans. With heavy losses, they withdrew to the U.S. side of the river and lost all hope of advancing farther. The other prong of this offensive, absent any coordination with the first, crossed from New York into Canada just west of the Hudson-Richelieu corridor. This effort was aborted after encountering dug-in defenders at the Battle of Chateaugay, barely across the Canadian border. The second winter of the war froze on a stalemate.

The pivotal event of 1813, however, occurred in October outside Leipzig, Germany, where the combined allies met the legions of France. For nearly a week, more than 500,000 men fought to bloody exhaustion. When the smoke cleared, Napoleon was in retreat. A year earlier, he had lost as large an army in Russia. This second loss ended his ability to call up another. France was out of men and confidence. By March 1814, the allies were in Paris. Napoleon had abdicated and gone into exile in Elba. While the situation in Europe remained volatile, the British clearly had the upper hand and were ready to send large reinforcements of both ships and men to North America.

YEAR OF CRISIS ON THE NIAGARA PENINSULA

As the summer campaigns of 1814 began, American prospects looked grim. The defeat of Napoleon allowed the British to reinforce Canada with veteran troops. Since the early defeats, the U.S. Army had been revitalized by the replacement of incompetent generals and the rise of younger officers such as Winfield Scott. Over the winter, Scott had drilled his men incessantly to achieve European professional standards. In July, American forces once again invaded Canada across the Niagara River but, after heavy fighting at Chippewa, Lundy's Lane and Fort Erie, were compelled to withdraw.

Meanwhile, the U.S. naval squadron sailed from Erie, carrying troops north to recapture Fort Mackinac at the northern end of Lake Huron. The attack failed, with heavy casualties ashore and the loss of two schooners. The expedition withdrew, and the Upper Lakes remained in British hands as a backwater of the war. On Lake Ontario, the naval stalemate continued. Both Chauncey and Yeo avoided decisive action while building ever-larger vessels to augment their fleets.

The Chesapeake Bay Campaign

In August 1814, a British expedition under Admiral Sir Alexander Cochrane carried four thousand troops under Major General Sir Robert Ross into Chesapeake Bay for an extended punitive raid. The primary objective was Baltimore, a wealthy city and the main nest of privateering. The purpose of the raid was to inflict enough hardship through destruction of property to persuade Americans to sue for peace. Norfolk was bypassed, having been stoutly defended in 1813. The British sailed up the Patuxent River in late August and began probing inland. Washington was burned (with restraint, the destruction confined to public buildings) as a target of opportunity after the British discovered the weakness of its defenses.

Yet the time spent against Washington granted Baltimore a reprieve to improve its defenses. After the burning of Washington, the militia and citizens of Baltimore grabbed their shovels with newfound zeal and made the dirt fly to surround the city with earthworks. It was not until early September that British troops were able to land below the city and fight the Americans at North Point. The British gained the field, at the expense of high casualties, but the Americans fell back to their earthworks. It was plain that any further action would prove even more costly to the British, who had come for a raid rather than a siege. When an overnight naval bombardment of Fort McHenry failed to open a water route into the city, the Americans gained a national anthem commemorating their defense. The British abandoned the attempt and withdrew from the Chesapeake.

Lake Champlain

As hard-pressed as the defenders of the Chesapeake shores felt, the most dangerous moment of the war for the United States took place at nearly

An Overview of the War of 1812

The bombardment of Fort McHenry, September 13–14, 1814, was the last episode of the Chesapeake campaign. The failure to take Baltimore discouraged the British government, and the commemoration of the defense in song gave the United States its national anthem. *Courtesy Library of Congress.*

the same time as the attack on Baltimore, but far to the north. By late August 1814, Lieutenant General Sir George Prevost had assembled 10,500 men, mostly veterans of the Peninsula War against the French. This force was poised to invade the United States along the Richelieu/Lake Champlain/Hudson River corridor, with the potential to threaten Albany if not New York City. This scenario had been attempted by the British during the American Revolution but had been stopped at the Battle of Saratoga (1777).

There was little but militia in the way to stop the British if they prevailed over the U.S. forces near the Canadian border. Worse yet, even if the British declined or failed to advance all the way to New York City yet remained a presence in Upstate New York, there was a chance that New England could be split from the rest of the country. The war had been unpopular in New England since it began. Some fought ardently, others brazenly traded with the enemy and most hoped merely to wait out the war. Had this British invasion succeeded, it is possible that the New England states would have made a separate peace and divided the union.

Historically, the north–south waterways of Lake Champlain and the Hudson River had dominated the strategic planning in the French and Indian Wars in addition to the American Revolution, being at once the most direct route from Montreal to New York and the means of isolating New England from the rest of the country. Plattsburgh Bay was the only good harbor at the north end of Lake Champlain, and U.S. commander Lieutenant Thomas Macdonough had anchored his squadron there, just east of the town, in an excellent defensive position. A north wind that would allow the British to sortie from their base would force them to beat to windward to get into the bay and attack.

One year and one day after the Battle of Lake Erie, and two days before the bombardment of Fort McHenry, on September 11, 1814, British lieutenant general Sir George Prevost attacked the American line south of Plattsburgh, while Royal Navy captain Robert Downie's squadron beat its way into the bay to attack Macdonough. The U.S. squadron remained at anchor, and by 0930 the British had anchored as well. A murderous stationary artillery duel followed. As at Lake Erie, the flagship, Macdonough's *Saratoga*, bore the brunt of enemy fire and suffered the highest casualties. British Captain Downie, however, was killed early in the battle, and by 1130 most of the British ships had surrendered and the rest fled.

When the smoke cleared, Prevost realized that he no longer had naval support. A more aggressive commander might have pressed on to destroy the small American army and might at least have occupied Plattsburgh. But Prevost declined to risk further casualties and withdrew into Canada. It was the naval battle of Plattsburgh Bay that turned aside the direst threat of the war. National deliverance has never hung on so slim a thread as it had on the anchor cables of Macdonough's battered ships.

THE SOUTHERN FRONTIER

While the scent of black powder hung heavy to the north, the year 1814 saw a fierce campaign waged against the Creek Indians in Alabama by U.S. general Andrew Jackson. This war within a war would likely have occurred irrespective of the causation of the War of 1812. The direct linkage is that Tecumseh had spent extensive time in the South preaching Indian unity and resistance to white encroachment. Militant young men who heeded Tecumseh were known as the Redsticks. In early 1814, they surprised Fort Mims and massacred several hundred whites, both military and civilian. A punitive campaign soon pushed south from Tennessee. The Creek War gave Andrew Jackson a winning reputation and command experience in time to lead the defense of the Gulf Coast. It was here that the British force, which had successfully raided the Chesapeake, next turned its attention.

The battle of Plattsburgh Bay, September 11, 1814. This U.S. naval victory at the northern end of Lake Champlain led to abandonment of an invasion by the strongest British force in the war, facing the least opposition on shore. *Macdonough's Victory on Lake Champlain*, engraved by B. Tanner. *Courtesy Library of Congress.*

Pensacola had been chosen as the initial destination, being a Spanish possession and hence a friendly port to the British, who had recently liberated Spain from the French. Jackson, however, had anticipated them. Despite Spain's neutrality, Jackson preemptively marched into Pensacola and overawed the small garrison without firing a shot. Denied a haven, the British sailed west with the objective of capturing New Orleans, arriving on the east side of the Mississippi Delta in early December. Unknown to both sides, across the Atlantic, months of peace negotiations were about to end the war.

Jackson rushed to take command of the defense, a motley force of regulars, green militia and paroled pirates. After some preliminary and indecisive engagements, the British, thoroughly miserable from a month camping in freezing swamps, decided for a major attack. On January 8, 1815, in the worst blunder of the war, British lieutenant general Sir Edward Packenham led 5,800 troops in a frontal assault against Jackson's 4,300 men occupying formidable earthworks and well supported by heavy artillery. In the ensuing slaughter, British casualties were 34 percent versus less than 2 percent among the Americans. New Orleans was the last major battle of the war.

News of this dramatic victory arrived in Washington almost together with word that a peace treaty had been signed by U.S. and British negotiators in Ghent, Belgium, three weeks earlier. It took several more months for ships at sea to get the word, and several ship-to-ship actions were fought in the spring of 1815. The last blood spilled was on June 30, more than three years after the declaration of war.

SUMMARY OF THE PEACE NEGOTIATIONS

If the Orders in Council (Britain's restrictive trade policies) had been repealed sooner and news of it reached Washington before war was declared, there would have been no war. The initial British position was to forego offensive action, hoping that the Americans would accept the status quo on other issues after their major grievance had been removed. A truce proposed by the governor of Upper Canada, Sir George Prevost, was readily accepted by U.S. commanders along the Ontario–St. Lawrence shore until sharp reprimands came from Washington reminding all that their assigned task was the conquest of Canada and that the time for peace negotiations was up to the government.

This was before the debacles on the front were known. By year's end, the Americans were wishing that they had been open to the overture. In 1813, the czar of Russia offered to mediate. His motives were not strictly humanitarian. Russia needed a strong Britain on the continent to help contain Napoleon and therefore did not want British strength sapped by a distant minor war. This time, the British, sensing that they had the upper hand, declined the czar's offer. By 1814, with Napoleon defeated and in exile, the British position was suddenly much stronger in terms of the resources they could bring to bear against the troublesome United States. The Americans recognized their danger as well and sent a team of five able negotiators—John Quincy Adams, Albert Gallatin, Henry Clay, James Bayard and Jonathan Russell—to Ghent, Belgium. There they met in late August to seek a peace with English diplomats Dr. William Adams, Henry Goulburn and Lord Gambier.

At first, the British position was to demand concessions, most notably forts along the American shores of the Great Lakes. Their primary motive was to guard against future invasions of Canada. The American negotiators were adamant against any cession of land. They sensed war weariness in the British and decided to wait them out. The talks dragged on through the fall, but when the news came of British failure to take Baltimore and their loss of the naval battle of Plattsburgh, New York, the Americans felt that time was on their side. They, in turn, had to give up on seeking redress for any of the stated causes of the war. The treaty that resulted, signed December on 24, 1814, was silent on the rights of neutrals to trade and on impressments, and it included pledges to respect Native American prewar boundaries.

Strictly speaking, there is nothing in the written record to indicate that the United States achieved any of its war aims, while the British aim was simply to hold Canada, which they did. The larger picture is that both sides grew a wary respect for each other. When Napoleon made his hundred-days comeback in 1815, the press gangs were out in force to recommission many Royal Navy vessels. They were very careful not to impress any Americans. It is hard to say if this policy would have persisted if Napoleon had been the victor at Waterloo.

When the United States took Indian lands, the British decided not to contest it. More importantly, when tensions arose over the U.S.-Canadian border, like the Maine–New Brunswick border dispute of 1839 or the Oregon boundary dispute of 1844, there was much saber rattling, but both sides sought negotiation. At the most basic level, the United States declared war on Great Britain in 1812 to gain respect and to force Britain to take it seriously. This was achieved, and in the bargain Americans learned to take themselves seriously.

BUILDING THE U.S. NAVAL SQUADRON ON LAKE ERIE

At dawn on July 17, 1812, the fifty-four men of the U.S. garrison at Fort Mackinac learned of the war through a surprise visit by three hundred British troops and Canadian militia from nearby St. Joseph Island, reinforced by several hundred Indians. The British asked for the keys to the fort and promptly got them. Daniel Dobbins, a merchant shipmaster hailing from Erie, was at Mackinac at the time and had his schooner, the *Salina*, commandeered as a cartel (an unarmed vessel designated to carry civilians or paroled prisoners of war) to evacuate civilians to Cleveland. Originally from Mifflin County in Pennsylvania, Dobbins had moved to Erie as a land surveyor at age nineteen and did not become a shipmaster until ten years later. Since sailing the lakes was by far the best way to travel in the region, Dobbins gradually learned seamanship and geography.

By the time of the war, he was thirty-six and had been navigating his own vessel on the lakes for six years. He had as thorough a knowledge of the geography of the Great Lakes as anyone of that era. Upon arriving at Detroit, Dobbins was detained by the U.S. Army because his vessel was deemed needed as a transport. A few weeks later, on August 16, Dobbins witnessed at Detroit nearly the same surrender scene as at Mackinac but on a larger scale. British general Isaac Brock used the threat that if the fort had to be taken by assault he might not be able to restrain his Indian allies in the aftermath. U.S. general William Hull surrendered a force of 2,500 men and all arms and equipment to an inferior force of British troops backed, however, by an indeterminate number of Indians. In the space of one month, the entire Northwest Territory had fallen into British and Indian hands.

Daniel Dobbins, merchant mariner. An Erie-based owner and shipmaster, Dobbins brought the first eyewitness accounts to Washington of the disastrous losses of Mackinac and Detroit in the summer of 1812. It was he who persuaded the secretary of the navy to authorize building the Lake Erie squadron at Erie, Pennsylvania. *Courtesy Erie County Historical Society.*

For a time, Dobbins feared for his life, having given his parole at Mackinac (a promise not to take up arms against his captors in exchange for his release). When the British took Detroit, Dobbins's act of staying with the *Salina* as a U.S. Army transport could have been seen as breaking parole and therefore making him liable to execution. Dobbins sought out Colonel Nichols, a British officer known to him, and asked for his protection. A few days later, Dobbins received a pass to take charge of three open boats to evacuate civilians and paroled soldiers to Cleveland.

The island-hopping journey took Dobbins three days. He arrived on August 22 and pressed on to Erie on the twenty-fourth, bringing first notice of the loss of Mackinac and Hull's capitulation at Detroit. General Meade, of the Pennsylvania militia, asked Dobbins to go to Washington and give a firsthand report to President Madison and his cabinet. On September 11, Dobbins met with President Madison and the entire cabinet to give them the first detailed report by an eyewitness to the debacle in the northwest. Immediately grasping the need for a naval force on Lake Erie, the cabinet asked Dobbins the best place to build, whereupon he stated Erie to be the only viable location. Five days later, on September 16, Dobbins received a commission as a sailing master in the U.S. Navy (refer to table of ranks in appendices). He returned to Erie with specifications for building gunboats and authority to spend $2,000, a token down payment on the eventual construction cost of the squadron.

Dobbins contracted boatbuilder Ebeneezer Crosby from Buffalo, New York, to begin building four gunboats at Lee's Run, now the foot of Myrtle Street in Erie. These gunboats were intended to carry one or two heavy guns

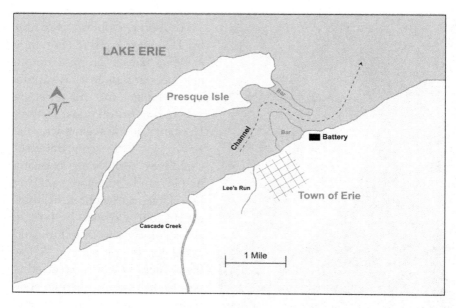

Map of Presque Isle Bay and the town of Erie, Pennsylvania, in 1813. The sandbars at the entrance prevented British ships from sailing in to attack but also required arduous efforts to get the large U.S. vessels out.

on pivot mounts near midships and followed several designs in use by the navy. The specification called for a vessel fifty feet between perpendiculars, by thirteen feet, six inches in beam and six feet, two inches in depth of hold, with a two-masted lateen rig. Dobbins knew that such a rig might do for rivers and estuaries but would be quite unsuitable for Lake Erie. The lateen rig has its virtues, most prominent of which is weatherliness, but the rig can be difficult to shorten down, especially with crews inexperienced in its use. Lake Erie is known for rapid increases in wind strength and wave height, and this puts a premium on being able to reef quickly. On his own initiative, Dobbins had the gunboats rigged as schooners.

At about the same time, USN captain Isaac Chauncey, then commandant of the New York Navy Yard, was appointed commander of the Great Lakes Theater of operations in September 1812. At age forty-one, Chauncey was one of the most senior U.S. naval officers and had extensive experience in ship construction and repair. He immediately established a base at Sackets Harbor, New York, at the eastern end of Lake Ontario. Chauncey contracted Henry Eckford, who had been his civilian chief constructor at the New York Navy Yard, to take charge of designing and supervising the

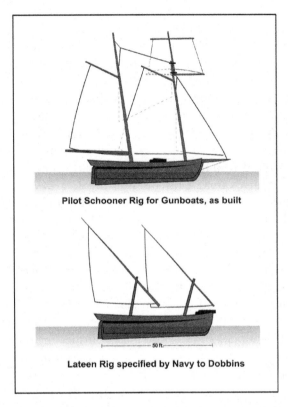

Pilot Schooner Rig for Gunboats, as built

50 ft

Lateen Rig specified by Navy to Dobbins

Dobbins returned to Erie as a sailing master in the U.S. Navy, with orders to build four gunboats. The navy specifications reflect both the Mediterranean origins of the type and ignorance of local conditions on Lake Erie. Fortunately for the United States, Dobbins exercised his own initiative in having the boats built to be rigged as schooners.

construction of the needed warships. Thirty miles to the north, the British began a reciprocal shipbuilding effort at Kingston, Ontario. For the next two and a half years, the contest on Lake Ontario was dubbed "the shipwright's war." Ever-larger ships were built by both sides in a frantic bid for naval superiority. Commanders on both sides recognized that defeat of their squadron would likely mean defeat of their nation in the war.

Lake Erie was a secondary priority. To address the need for a naval force there, Chauncey sent Lieutenant Jesse Duncan Elliott in September 1812 to improvise a naval station at Black Rock, adjacent to Buffalo, New York, on the Niagara River. Elliott lost no time making an impression on both sides. On the night of October 9, he led a daring raid, a "cutting out party," to seize two British vessels lying at anchor close to the Canadian shore, under the guns of shore batteries in the Niagara River. One was the former American schooner *John Adams*, captured at Detroit and renamed HMS *Detroit*. The other was the armed brig *Caledonia*.

Elliott's two open boats rowed several miles in the deepest black of a chilly night and in strict silence. Detection would bring fire from both muskets and cannons. The American surprise was complete enough that after clambering on board with sword and pistol, there was little bloodshed before the British crews had surrendered. But there was enough shouting and shooting to alert the shore battery. In haste, the Americans raised sail, cut the anchor cables and got underway before the guns ashore found their mark. Elliott managed to get the *Caledonia* to Black Rock, but the *Detroit* was run ashore on Grand Island and burned to prevent recapture. For his courage and initiative, Elliott received a medal and a sword from Congress. During the winter of 1812–13, the *Caledonia* was one of five small merchant vessels that the Americans converted to gunboats. British guns across the river at Fort Erie blocked access to the lake. The vessels could not be moved unless the Americans first took the British fort.

Meanwhile, back in Erie, Pennsylvania, Dobbins was in an awkward position. The secretary of the navy had ordered him to build gunboats there but had also attached him to Chauncey's command. Dobbins wrote to Chauncey and copied Elliott, requesting the forwarding of stores. Elliott, who as a lieutenant outranked Dobbins, immediately dismissed the idea of building at Erie. Dobbins pressed on at Erie, claiming to have never received an order from Chauncey to join Elliott at Black Rock. Left to choose between Black Rock and Erie as the place to concentrate effort, Chauncey decided to make a personal inspection.

New Year's Day 1813 found Chauncey and Eckford in Erie, inspecting the work in progress. They deemed the gunboats too small and ordered the two that were not yet planked to be lengthened ten feet. They stayed a single day and then returned to Black Rock with no other decisions firm. By January 9, however, Chauncey had ordered Dobbins to begin cutting timber for a large brig, and by month's end timber for a second brig had been ordered as well. The preceding October, Chauncey had ordered timber for the same-sized vessels be prepared at Black Rock. Having seen both sites in person, Chauncey, perhaps guided by Eckford, deemed Erie the better site. Elliott soon had other duties, as Chauncey recognized that he was better utilized as a commanding officer on board Chauncey's flagship, the *Madison*.

It was clear to both Chauncey and Eckford that a much greater level of effort would be needed to have serviceable ships on Lake Erie in 1813. Some weeks later, while briefly back in New York City, Chauncey contracted with shipbuilder Noah Brown to take a crew to Erie and take charge of the shipbuilding. Brown, Eckford and Chauncey were well known to one another through prewar work at the New York Navy Yard. Eckford has often been credited with the design of the Lake Erie naval vessels, but this is incorrect. Although a capable and prolific designer, Eckford had his hands more than full building the Lake Ontario squadron. Chauncey's contract letter to Brown makes no mention of building to draughts or specifications

Jesse Duncan Elliott, promoted from lieutenant to master commandant for his daring cutting-out raid in October of 1812 during which he captured two vessels from under the guns of Fort Erie on the Niagara River. Elliott was a technically competent professional, but throughout his career he showed a particular talent for alienating those around him. *Captn. J.D. Elliott*, by David Edwin, engraver. *Courtesy Library of Congress.*

to be received from Eckford. Instead, Chauncey's February 18 contract letter read, in part:

> *I wish you to proceed with all possible dispatch for Erie…and there build in the shortest time possible 2 Brigs capable of mounting 18-32 pdr carronades & 2 long 9's. These vessels must be so constructed that they can be made to draw not exceeding 6½ or 7 feet water; and at the same time possess the qualities of sailing fast and bearing their guns with ease. Their frame & will be left entirely to yourself.*

This last sentence contains a key phrase: the "frame &" ("&" meaning "etc.") determines the shape of the ship, which Chauncey left up to Brown. The contract letter was a performance specification describing required characteristics for the brigs but leaving all design decisions to Brown. Three days after accepting the job, Brown set out for Erie with a gang of fifteen shipwrights to whom he had promised a wage of two dollars per day. This was twice the shipyard rate in New York and an indication of the expected difficulties in the job ahead.

Just getting there was a journey of 450 frozen miles requiring fourteen days of travel. Their route took them first up the shore of the Hudson River to Albany, then west through the Mohawk River Valley and finally down the shores of Lakes Ontario and Erie. Arriving at Erie on March 6, 1813,

Noah Brown found a small snowbound frontier town of five hundred souls and immediately recognized the true scope of the job. Dobbins and Crosby had by then finished planking the two smaller gunboats, but they had not yet caulked them. The second pair were barely more than keel assemblies. Enough timber had been cut to lay the keels and to begin framing the large brigs. But before these could be built, barracks, a smithy, storehouses and a sail loft all had to be built of logs and a much larger workforce hired. While Brown ran the shipyard, Dobbins became the master of procurement, using his knowledge of the countryside to find supplies and arrange transport.

Eventually, the workforce grew to about two hundred, but by that time the work was at least halfway along. The whole force worked with astonishing rapidity, "each man working as if on a strife." The shipbuilding effort at Erie exemplified what today would be called "emergency wartime construction," or "we need it yesterday." To build the log buildings, six vessels, fourteen boats, several dozen gun carriages and four cameling scows within six months and working entirely with hand tools was an impressive feat. Brown summed it up: "[P]lain work is all that is wanted. They [the ships] are only needed for one battle. If we win that is all that is wanted of them. If we lose they are good enough to be captured."

The two small gunboats were named *Porcupine* and *Tigress*. The pair that Chauncey and Eckford ordered lengthened became the *Scorpion* and the *Ariel*. The *Ariel* was later described as a New York pilot boat model and was noticeably the fastest vessel on the lake at the time. The inference is that *Ariel* and *Scorpion* were not sisters, although *Scorpion* had enough speed to keep up with *Ariel* and ahead of the large brigs at the head of Perry's battle line. These two schooners, being longer than the others, would be faster in any case, but since they were not very far along when Brown arrived, he had the opportunity to make significant design changes.

The six vessels were built at two different sites over a mile apart. The gunboats *Scorpion*, *Porcupine* and *Tigress* were built at the mouth of Lee's Run, which was directly below the bluff on which the town was situated and a short walk from available lodging. The two large brigs and the *Ariel* were built at the mouth of Cascade Creek, a mile and a quarter west of Lee's Run. To better supervise its construction, Brown moved *Ariel* from the Lee's run site to the Cascade Creek yard where he built the brigs. This would not have been practical if the vessel had progressed beyond a backbone assembly. The decision to build the two large brigs required a site with deeper water than at Lee's Run. Cascade Creek runs steeply down into the harbor. Today, alterations to the landscape such as piers have diverted the mouth into a

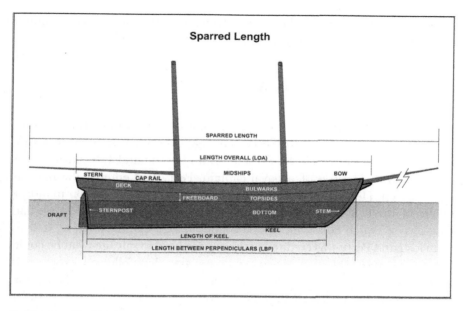

Profile view of sailing ship, showing the defining terminology.

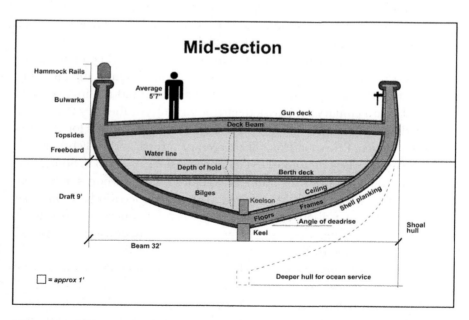

Midsection of Niagara, showing terminology. Also note on lower right the use of a dashed line to show the greater depth of hold that would be required for ocean service.

shallow delta, but in 1813, the creek's unrestricted flow would have scoured a deep basin at its mouth, giving Brown the depth he needed.

PERRY ARRIVES AT ERIE

In the midst of this frenetic chopping, sawing and hammering, Master Commandant Oliver Hazard Perry, then age twenty-seven, arrived in Erie late in the day on March 26 to establish and command U.S. naval forces on Lake Erie. The son of a naval captain, Perry had entered the navy at age fourteen. He had served as a lieutenant in frigates and as commanding officer of the U.S. schooner *Revenge* in peacetime. His ship, the *Revenge*, had wrecked on Watch Hill Reef, Rhode Island, in fog in January 1811. No lives were lost, and Perry was credited with working hard to salvage what he could from the wreck. The obligatory court-martial that followed exonerated Perry, ascribing the loss chiefly to navigational error by a civilian pilot. Despite retaining his rank and commission, the career of any commander who lost a ship, for any reason less than having it shot out from under him, was tainted for years afterward, if not forever. Perry survived to command a gunboat squadron based in Newport, Rhode Island, albeit not a seagoing command. As war became imminent, Perry petitioned for service at sea, but an assignment (let alone a command) eluded him.

In November 1812, Perry wrote to Chauncey, volunteering for the lakes as the most likely place to see action. Chauncey had his hands full initiating a large-scale shipbuilding effort on Lake Ontario and did not immediately respond, but in a January 21, 1813 letter to the secretary of the navy, Chauncey requested Perry's transfer. From the outset, Chauncey intended for Perry to establish the Lake Erie squadron. The secretary agreed, and on February 11, orders arrived for Perry to report to Chauncey at Sackets Harbor. Soon after, Perry and 150 men from his gunboat squadron left Newport for Sackets Harbor. Three weeks later, they arrived at the bleak, iced-in base on Lake Ontario. Perry's first disappointment came when Chauncey assigned most of Perry's Newport men to fill out his own crews, foreshadowing what would become a major source of friction as the year progressed.

Chauncey wrote orders on March 15, 1813, sending Perry on to Erie with a small contingent of twenty-five men. The orders included details of procurement arrangements made to date but left much to Perry's discretion. By the time Perry arrived in Erie, Noah Brown had the keels of both brigs laid and the frames were going up. The two smaller gunboats were awaiting

Oliver Hazard Perry, master commandant, USN. The son of a U.S. frigate captain, and in the service from age twelve, Perry was brave, forceful, hardworking and resourceful but also impetuous and prone to fits of temper that were fortunately very short-lived. A charismatic leader, his men suffered horrific casualties during the battle, but morale never failed. Engraved by J.B. Forrest from the original by J.W. Jarvis. *Courtesy Library of Congress.*

caulking, but little had been done on the second pair. Perry assumed the duties of both station and squadron commander. As master commandant (equivalent to commander today), his rank was a grade below captain and a grade above lieutenant, which was a grade over sailing master. He brought with him management experience from supervising the construction and organization of the gunboat squadron in Newport. Dobbins, Brown and Perry formed a complementary team. All three were men of tremendous energy who, just as importantly, recognized one another's merits. Perry had the sense to leave Brown to what he did best, and alongside Dobbins Perry threw himself into the task of plugging the considerable gaps in procurement of men and materiel.

PROCUREMENT PROBLEMS

Within three days of arriving in Erie, Perry had set off on a journey to Pittsburgh to arrange contracts for equipment. Already a city of forges, foundries and coal smoke, Pittsburgh's companies were able to manufacture the shot, anchors, stoves and most of the cordage needed for the Lake Erie squadron. Sailcloth had to come from Philadelphia. Some of the guns were sent from Sackets Harbor, but most were cast in Georgetown, adjacent to Washington, D.C., and shipped overland. Getting enough iron to Erie for fastenings and miscellaneous hardware proved a constant problem until the ships were nearly completed. Most of the surviving correspondence from the winter building effort relates to the logistical problems of locating supplies and arranging delivery.

By April 11, Perry was back in Erie, where he found that Purser Samuel Hambleton and Sailing Master William Vigeron Taylor, in charge of thirty hands, had arrived during his absence. Hambleton had been Perry's purser in the Newport gunboat squadron and was a friend and confidant of Perry's for years afterward. Taylor had been a master of merchant ships before the war. He had joined the navy in Newport, where he served in Perry's gunboat squadron. At age forty-one, Taylor's maturity and experience were greatly prized by Perry. Perry sent Taylor to Pittsburgh to oversee manufacture of cordage and obtain other items.

By April 23, Perry was able to report to Chauncey that the brigs were nearly planked and that the two small gunboats, the *Tigress* and *Porcupine*, had been launched. As weather permitted, boats were dispatched to Buffalo to obtain tar, oakum and gunpowder. The most critical material shortage was iron for fastenings. Dobbins scoured the countryside as far away as Bellefonte, Pennsylvania, two hundred miles from Erie. Eventually, enough iron was obtained, but the lack of a ready supply in midwinter slowed construction.

The majority of Dobbins's papers from this period are orders and receipts for procurement of needed materiel and services: powder and cannons from Buffalo, cordage and shot from Pittsburgh and items from local sources such as wagon loads of bricks for a steambox and blacksmith forges, provisions and boarding bills, bushels of coal and shaped spars, not to mention dozens of labor receipts for "days in the woods getting timber." A timber survey done on the wreck of the *Niagara* in 1913 listed species used in construction of the hull as red, black and white oak, as well as cherry, chestnut and poplar, with cedar and pine being used to plank the bulwarks. The need for speed meant that the selection process was the nearest large tree, then the one behind it and then the next beyond that. One of these contracts becomes important later: a deposit to John Greenwood dated February 24, 1813 (found in the Dobbins Papers, box 5, at the Erie County Historical Society):

Received of Daniel Dobbins thirty six dollars and seventy five cents in part pay for a contract of oars and sweeps for the gunboats. [The specific order was]...*for sixty sweeps 20 to 25 ft long, and fifty oars 14 ft long. Sweeps to be 6" thick in the loom, 9" blade width, blade thickness 2" the oars were to be 4" thick in the loom, have 6" blade width by 1" thick...* [Two weeks later, the receipt is issued:] *Delivered 8 March 1813 sixty sweeps and fifty oars, received ninety two dollars and twenty five cents.*

Wooden shipbuilding. A large vessel in frame and partially planked, giving some idea of how much wood had to be felled and sawn by hand. *Sir Isaac Brock. Courtesy Metropolitan Toronto Reference Library, J. Robert Ross Collection.*

The two large brigs needed eighteen sweeps each, and each was twenty-five feet long. That would account for thirty-six sweeps. If the remaining twenty-four were twenty feet long, there would have been six each for the schooner gunboats, which is workable for vessels of this size. There may have been some available from existing inventory to bring the numbers up for the smaller vessels. The oars would have gone to the ship's boats, at four to eight per boat. The full inventory of boats for the squadron is not known, but we know that Brown built fourteen boats and that others may have been available for local purchase or may have come with the gunboats from Black Rock.

Due to the shortage of oakum, the below-waterline seams of the *Niagara* and *Lawrence* were partially caulked with sheet lead. Perry was also aware that the brigs' shoal draft and heavy armament would make for marginal stability if stone ballast were used or even iron, so he used lead ingots for internal ballast. The secretary of the navy later complained of Perry being extravagant with the "public purse" in purchasing lead in lieu of the more common stone.

To this Perry replied, correctly, that the brigs were too shallow to carry stone ballast and that denser material was needed to stow sufficient weight in the space available. The secretary of the navy accepted Perry's explanation, but the fact that an explanation was required indicates that the brigs were of a nonstandard design and that no drawings of the ships existed in Washington. An attempt was made to launch the first of the two brigs on May 24, but it stuck on the ways. Finally, by June 4, 1813, both brigs were afloat.

INVASION OF THE NIAGARA PENINSULA

Meanwhile, Perry was called to assist Chauncey with removing the British from their forts on the Niagara River. On May 24, Perry sailed overnight from Erie in a four-oared cutter, arriving at Buffalo the next evening. From there, he hired a horse and rode overland to the mouth of the Niagara River, joining Chauncey just in time, literally, to assist in the invasion of the Niagara Peninsula. The night of the twenty-sixth saw Chauncey and Perry directing boat crews in taking soundings and setting buoys close inshore to guide the invasion vessels, both the gunboat schooners to provide fire support and the boats carrying troops to the beach.

At daylight the next morning, on May 27, 1813, Perry came under fire for the first time in his career while directing close-in shore bombardment from the guns of the U.S. Navy schooners supporting the amphibious assault. The landings were opposed, and the schooners, under Perry's direction, closed to within grapeshot range, exposed to countering fire and at no small risk of running aground, to pour heavy cover fire into the defending ranks just ahead of the landing craft.

Upon hitting the beach, the Americans swarmed ashore and forced the defenders back with heavy volleys of musket fire. As the British retreated inland, the gunboats kept up the pressure, switching to round shot and elevating their guns to fire over the heads of the landing force. The landing operation was highly successful, inflicting heavy casualties on the defenders. Forced to abandon Forts George and Erie, at north and south ends of the Niagara River, respectively, the British retreated toward Burlington (now Hamilton Ontario).

MOVING THE BLACK ROCK SHIPS TO ERIE

With both sides of the river now in American hands, the five small ships at Black Rock were free to move into Lake Erie. These were the brig *Caledonia*,

Building the U.S. Naval Squadron on Lake Erie

Amphibious assault on Fort George, May 27, 1813. Perry was close inshore directing covering fire for the troops rowing in to make an opposed landing. *The Taking of Fort George* from *The Battle of Fort George*, by Ernest Cruikshank. *Courtesy Project Gutenburg.*

the sloop *Trippe* and the schooners *Somers*, *Ohio* and *Amelia*. The next day, May 28, Chauncey ordered Perry and fifty-five seamen to finish fitting them out and deliver them to Erie, a task that took nearly three weeks. Even when the little squadron was ready, there was one more serious obstacle: the two miles of river between the Black Rock yard and the open lake. The north-flowing current was too strong to be stemmed under sail by anything less than an opposing northerly gale—not likely in June. The alternative was to run lines ashore and drag the vessels along the riverbank.

Fortunately, Perry was authorized to seek assistance from the army in getting out of the river, if necessary, and it plainly was. Overcoming the strong current in the Niagara River required two hundred soldiers and several teams of oxen. It took five days to move the vessels from Black Rock to the open lake. The two companies of infantry were retained to man the squadron for the passage to Erie. Exhaustion made the men more vulnerable to sickness, and many, including Perry himself, were suffering from fever. The tiny squadron got underway on June 13, but heavy westerly winds drove it back to anchorage in the mouth of Buffalo Creek. By the next day, the winds had calmed, and Perry weighed anchor and sailed out again. This time, the weather was very light, with shifting headwinds. Light air was just as well considering that on this passage 80 percent of the crews were soldiers rather than sailors.

While sailing to Erie, the Americans came close to disaster without even being aware of it. The British squadron, which at the time outgunned the

Americans, was looking for Perry and his ships. Near Dunkirk, New York, an observer on shore had both squadrons in sight, but due to fog on the lake, the two forces did not see each other. Perry's famous luck held, and after a tediously slow passage of five days to cover one hundred miles, all five vessels arrived in Erie on June 19. The light air probably also averted a loss to foundering. The schooner *Amelia* leaked so badly that upon arrival at Erie it was condemned as unfit for use and never sailed again. In the nearly four weeks that Perry had been away, Brown had been driving the work along, and all of the six vessels were nearing completion.

NAMING THE BRIGS

Sad news arrived in Erie on July 12. The previous month, the U.S. frigate *Chesapeake* sailed out of Boston and was captured by the HMS *Shannon* after a brief but fierce battle. Casualties had been heavy, including USN captain James Lawrence. As the mortally wounded Lawrence was carried below, he exhorted his men, "Don't give up the ship!" His example of defiant courage was all that the United States could salvage from the loss. Coming on the heels of a string of U.S. naval victories, this news stunned the nation. Perry directed his officers to wear black armbands for three weeks.

On July 19, Perry received an order from the secretary of the navy directing him to name one of the two brigs *Niagara*, in honor of the recent successful invasion of the Niagara Peninsula, and the other brig *Lawrence*. Naming the smaller vessels was left to Perry's discretion. He chose the *Lawrence* as his flagship and, at the suggestion of Purser Hambleton, further honored Captain Lawrence by secretly (flown only on the day of the battle) commissioning a battle flag with the dying words of Captain James Lawrence as a motto, "Don't Give Up the Ship." It is ironic that these words, now associated with Perry's victory, originated from a defeat.

As summer wore on, there were still critical shortages that delayed the squadron. The two brigs needed to be moored to pilings driven in the harbor bottom because the anchors and cables ordered from Pittsburgh were late in delivery. For weeks, the British squadron had been appearing intermittently near the entrance to Presque Isle Bay, Erie's harbor, but it could not force an entrance due to the bar. On July 21, Royal Navy commander R.H. Barclay closed in a little too close for comfort, and Perry ordered three of the gunboats to get underway and drive them off. A few shots were exchanged without effect, until Barclay withdrew.

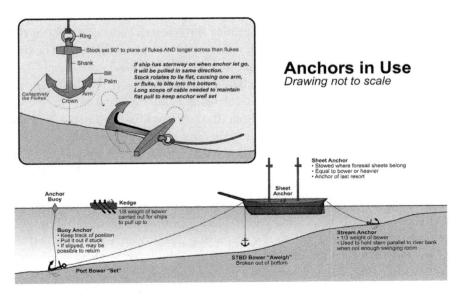

Anchors were among the most vital equipment on board, the last resort to keep a ship from being blown ashore. The sketch shows the various uses for anchors of different relative sizes. An anchor that might be the bower for a brig like *Niagara* might only serve as a stream anchor on a frigate or a kedge on a ship of the line. In this era, chain cable was not yet in widespread use. Achieving good holding and protecting a hemp cable from chafe required constant attention.

The next day, Perry went on board the *Scorpion* and directed several shots over the peninsula at the British vessels. On the twenty-fifth, *Queen Charlotte* fired toward the militia camp and then sailed off before the gunboats could sally. On the twenty-seventh, Barclay again closed and exchanged fire with the American gunboats at long range, with no hits for either side. Barclay's ships had appeared for part of every day between the twenty-first and the twenty-seventh. Perry couldn't get his ships over the bar with the British squadron poised to strike, but he knew that he needed to be ready the instant that an opportunity presented itself. Finally, the day came when the British left Erie uncovered, probably because they needed to reprovision.

CAMELING OVER THE BAR

As arduous as the task of getting the ships out of Black Rock had been, an even greater effort was required to get the squadron out of Erie. The harbor, better known as Presque Isle Bay, was enclosed and protected by a seven-mile-long sand spit peninsula, with the sole entrance at its eastern end. A sandbar of two ridges lay across this entrance, with a limiting depth of six feet under normal conditions. Even for vessels of shallow draft, the channel was S-shaped and required approaching very close to land on which defensive gun batteries had been built. The saving grace of this challenging shoal was that it gave protection to the squadron while it was being built. It was impossible for Barclay to simply sail into the harbor and attack while he had the superior force.

But now, what had kept the British out was keeping the Americans in. The existence of the bar had been factored in from the outset, and Noah Brown had planned and built what he needed for "cameling," or lifting the two large brigs over the bar. Nautical camels are containers, or barges, that are partially flooded before being secured along both sides of a ship. Pumping out the camels causes them to rise, imparting the buoyancy needed to lift the vessel to which they are attached. The camels built by Noah Brown's crew were simple boxy barges, not recorded in any detail.

According to Brown's son, writing years later, four barges, or "skows," were built. An 1860 letter from Sailing Master Stephen Champlin gives dimensions of fifty feet long, ten feet at the beam and eight feet in depth. These dimensions are about right for the lifting capacity required. The camels were towed out and, once secured alongside the brigs with lines, flooded until perhaps a foot of freeboard remained. Then beams were inserted through the sweep ports of the brigs and blocked against the decks of the camels. As the camels were emptied of water, their buoyancy would bring the ship up with them. Though the British squadron's departure gave Perry the military opportunity to cross the bar, the weather now sought to deny him. Several days of easterly wind had pushed the lake level up at the western end while lowering the water depth at Erie. Instead of the usual six feet, the bar had only four and a half feet of water over it, half the loaded draft of the *Lawrence*. Perry and his men knew that they would be facing a struggle.

The original log of the *Lawrence*, the only known surviving squadron logbook, is at the Newport Historical Society in Newport, Rhode Island. The following chronology is taken from a transcript of the log prepared by late PHMC historian Robert Eaton.

At 0500 on Saturday, the *Lawrence* hove short and began to get underway, coming to anchor abreast the town at 0900. The wind being easterly, the passage of under two miles took close to four hours. Very likely the ship was kedged. The rest of the day went into lightening the ship, and by 2000 (8:00 p.m.), the camels had been brought alongside, and the men worked far into the night, "all hands employed in lashing and sinking the skows." On Sunday,

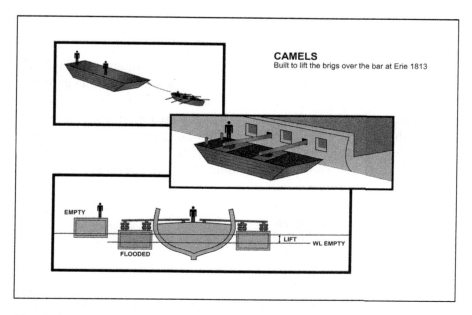

Cameling over the bar. The use of camels to lift vessels over sandbars goes back at least to sixteenth-century Holland. The need for them at Presque Isle had been known from the start. The genius of Noah Brown lay in the simplicity of his version of camels.

August 1, the *Lawrence* got underway at 0600 and soon grounded the stem in six feet, ten inches of water. At this time, they began to pump out the camels to lift the ship. The sheet and stream anchors were placed on board the schooner *Scorpion* and carried ahead by it. Once an anchor was set, the capstan was manned to heave the ship ahead. The buoyancy imparted by the camels took much of the weight but not all, and the keel cut a furrow through the sand as the taut anchor cable groaned and thrummed with vibration.

At 1300, six guns were sent ashore to further lighten the ship. By 1800, they had gotten over the first ridge and were anchored in three fathoms (eighteen feet). A few hours rest was all Perry dared allow.

At 0300 on August 2, a Monday, all hands had been called to offload eight more of the guns. By 0900, the *Lawrence* was again hove aground on the second, or outer ridge of the bar, in "six feet seven inches water." At 1100, the *Scorpion* again came alongside to carry the brig's anchors ahead. After two hours of effort, it was decided to reposition the scows to see if any more lift could be had. The men toiled on, and the brig moved at an agonizingly slow pace, again cutting a furrow over the sands with the keel. Inch by inch, the ship was dragged forward through the night until by

0700 on Tuesday, August 3, the work was getting easier, with the shallowest part of the bar behind them.

By 0900, the *Lawrence* rested at anchor in three fathoms of water, this time in the outer harbor. The crew immediately turned to getting guns and ballast back on board. The work continued on August 4, with provisioning and ammunition stowage. Until the *Lawrence* was rearmed, and restowed, it was as vulnerable as a molted lobster. The whole process was immediately repeated for the *Niagara*. No doubt the experience factor helped the second time around. More importantly, the water level was rising back to normal level. The *Niagara* was gotten over the bar in one day, on August 5, and by the sixth it had its guns back and stores loaded. The smaller vessels were worked over the bar without the camels.

MANNING THE SQUADRON

As great as were the problems of building the squadron, manning proved an even more daunting challenge. The single most important factor in the effectiveness of any ship is the crew. The squadron would be useless without enough trained men to man it, a problem shared by both sides on Lake Erie. Furthermore, it would be impossible to train new men to sail, let alone fight, without at least a core of professionals. These arrived in woefully small numbers throughout the spring and summer of 1813.

On March 30, Sailing Master William Taylor, two midshipmen and twenty seamen arrived in Erie. Perry had requested Taylor be assigned to accompany him to the lakes in a letter to the secretary of the navy on February 21 just as he left Newport. Following is a summary of the small detachments that trickled in:

> *26 March, Master Commandant O.H. Perry, and 25 seamen*
> *30 March, Sailing Master William. V. Taylor and 22 men*
> *17 April, Lt. Thomas Holdup, and 40 seamen*
> *5 May, Lt. John Brooks and 14 marines*
> *19 June, Perry's arrival from Black Rock with 5 vessels, 2 officers, 55 seamen. The 200 infantry assigned to temporary duty to fill out the crews were recalled to Buffalo after arrival in Erie.*
> *24 July, Sailing Master Stephen Champlin, 3 midshipmen, and 65 seamen*
> *31 July, 2 midshipmen, master's mate, and 51 seamen*
> *9 August, Master Commandant Jesse D. Elliott, 11 officers, and 91 seamen*

Building the U.S. Naval Squadron on Lake Erie

The sources tally 348 men of all ranks but do not represent a complete list. At least sixty militiamen signed on in Erie for the campaign, and on August 31, another 136 men from General Harrison's army volunteered for naval service. The exact number of men serving under Perry is uncertain. The best source is Purser Samuel Hambleton's "Prize List," which contains 532 names eligible for prize money. Of these, 248 were seamen, and another 124 were officers or petty officers, for a total of 372 naval personnel. The authorized complement for a twenty-gun brig was 170 of all ranks. The total complement to fully man the entire squadron to naval establishment would have been 740. It appears that everyone recognized that this level of manning was not realistic to expect, hence the requests for lesser numbers. The "Prize List" of 532 represents 71 percent of establishment.

Perry had been corresponding with General Harrison, who was pressing him to know when the squadron would be ready to assist the army and informed Perry of the second British attack on Fort Meigs. These letters were a great frustration to Perry, as the squadron was not ready yet. Perry wrote to Secretary of the Navy Jones on July 23, informing him of the British squadron hovering off Erie and of steady progress in the delivery of supplies but none in gaining personnel. He concluded, "I cannot describe to you Sir, the mortification of my situation. I have not heard that any seamen have yet left Sacketts Harbor for this place, as soon as they arrive, we shall meet the enemy—he is now off the harbor with six sail."

The very next day, on July 24, Sailing Master Stephen Champlin arrived with three midshipmen and sixty five seamen. As new men and officers arrived, Perry was frequently juggling assignments to make the best use of the available experience. By this time, Perry had been working long hours in a difficult situation for fully five months, and his correspondence reflects irritability and strain. He is constantly complaining to both Chauncey and Secretary of the Navy Jones about the lack of men and the experience level of those he has. Many of his officers held "acting" appointments to a higher grade than they officially held. In fact, the young officers assigned to Perry were as promising as any in the navy.

Champlin brought the largest single reinforcement Perry had yet seen, but feeling administratively overwhelmed and stretched thin with worry and fatigue, Perry was not satisfied and let his quick temper get the better of him. Three days later, on July 27, Perry wrote to Secretary of the Navy Jones complaining of the recent arrivals: "Very few of the men are seaman. I am rejoiced to have them, as bad as they are; we are ready to sail the instant officers and men arrive." Three days later, Perry sent off a follow-up: "I cannot but hope Comr. Chauncey will send me officers of some experience as I have not now officers enough <u>even</u> to navigate the <u>vessels</u>."

Writing directly to the secretary of the navy to complain about his immediate superior was a breach of protocol likely to have gotten Perry relieved of command were it not for his being so badly needed in such a remote station. Then, to make matters worse, Perry wrote to Chauncey and instead of thanking him for at last heeding his pleas, Perry dug himself in deeper by further complaint: "[T]he men that came by Mr. Champlin are a motley set, blacks, Soldiers, and boys, I cannot think that you saw them after they were selected. I am however pleased to see anything in the shape of a man."

These rash letters, surly and whining at the same time and in defiance of the chain of command, came back to haunt Perry a few days later. The letter to Chauncey, in particular, has often been cited in criticism of Perry as racist, which by present-day standards is true. The words are clearly disparaging, but there is nothing to indicate that Perry was any more or less racist than the overwhelming majority of his contemporaries in or out of uniform. The letter was mainly expressing frustration at the inadequacy of his reinforcements in regards to both number and quality. It would only be natural that an officer on Lake Ontario, when ordered to send men away, would choose the least experienced or least healthy. Perry was certainly accustomed to having mixed races on board.

It is known that many of Perry's crew were black, but just how many cannot be determined because muster rolls did not list race. The official policy was to limit recruitment to free white males. Each commander, however, was responsible for recruiting for his own ship. The obvious choice when confronted with a need to man the ship was recruit whoever was qualified and available but avoid any objections from higher up by not making any mention of race. As established by Dr. Jeffrey Bolster in his book *Black Jacks*, the national average was 20 percent of enlisted men being nonwhite. Even if applied to the Lake Erie squadron, the overall percentage would be lower, perhaps 10–15 percent, because officers and warrant officers were exclusively white. Ship's surgeon Usher Parsons recalled in later years that "about one in eight or one in twelve were black."

What can be said is that black seamen served in all theaters of the war, often with distinction. Those who served at Lake Erie, while perhaps the second choices of the Lake Ontario squadron, were probably among the more experienced seamen from the prewar regular navy and thus made a significant contribution to this campaign where trained seamen were in short supply. The Royal Navy also recruited free blacks, and part of the Canadian defense along the Niagara Peninsula was the "Colored Regiment," many of whom were runaway slaves from the United States. Thus African Americans served on both sides in this conflict, but identification of individuals has proved difficult.

In the meantime, the work of organizing the squadron with what talent was available continued. Purser Humphrey Magrath arrived in early July and was assigned to the *Niagara* and Purser Samuel Hambleton to the *Lawrence*, with additional responsibility as squadron Purser. Perry's next written order came three days later, on July 27, addressed to Purser Magrath: "I accept the offer of your services, to prepare the *Caledonia* for immediate service and request you will go on board and take charge of her." Clearly, Magrath had volunteered, and this unusual assignment calls attention to an unusual career.

Magrath had entered the navy as a midshipman and in due course received a lieutenant's commission. After the Barbary War, however, the navy was drastically downsized. Many officers were discharged, and those kept on had exceedingly dim prospects for promotion. Magrath made the unusual choice of resigning his commission and then reenlisting in the lesser rank of purser, the ship's accountant and purchasing agent.

Purser was a warrant position from which there would be no promotion, but there was opportunity for profit. Pursers were permitted an allowance of up to 7.5 percent for wastage, to enable them to build a reserve against contingencies. The purser also had a monopoly on providing the crew with "slops," purchasable items such as clothing beyond initial uniform allowance, soap, tobacco, sewing kits and so forth, for which he was allowed a 5 percent profit. Prudence in purchasing stores and in husbanding the wastage allowance were key to both the success of a given voyage and to personal fortune. It tells us something about Magrath that in an age that prized honor so highly he would eschew the potential for higher honor in command of a vessel for the more lucrative role of purser. In today's parlance, Magrath was pretty clearly someone who thought a lot about "taking care of number one." Living aft in the wardroom and not standing a watch but frequently having reason to confer with the captain, pursers sometimes became confidants of their captains despite the disparity in rank.

Under normal circumstances, no captain would consider going shorthanded in the purchasing and accounting department (for which accounts the captain was ultimately responsible) and, if short of deck officers, would rather make an acting promotion from among the deck department. Indeed, Perry was very short of officers, and Magrath did have thorough training in seamanship. Magrath may have offered to take command from genuinely patriotic motives, recognizing that seamanship was more important than accounting just then. Or he may have calculated that the commander of a vessel would get a much higher share of prize money than the purser.

When Perry reported these assignments to Chauncey and the secretary of the navy, he received a remonstrance from Secretary William Jones that it was against regulations for a purser to command any government vessel under any circumstances and that Magrath was to be removed at once. Perry had no choice but to reassign Magrath as purser of the *Niagara*.

By the end of July, the squadron was ready, barely, to end the shipyard phase of fitting out and make the shift to becoming operational. This is a psychological shift as much as a physical or administrative one. A ship in yard for repairs or fitting out is generally filthy and cluttered, with tools and materials scattered about, numerous craftsmen hurrying to get their jobs done and the yard manager needed to referee the right of way, as well as offering a din of tools and voices. A ship in commission is what we think of as "shipshape," clean and everything in its place.

On July 30, Perry gave all notice to have themselves and their baggage on board their assigned vessels by the thirty-first and thereafter to remain on board. It was time to get underway, beginning with the ordeal of cameling the *Lawrence* over the bar between July 31 and August 4.

Across the lake in the British camp, conditions were even more difficult, owing to the reality that the British isolation from a reliable supply of men and materiel was even greater than for the Americans. Commander Robert Herriot Barclay, the same age as Perry, had similarly gone to sea as a boy, in his case at age twelve. He had, however, seen a great deal more action. As a nineteen-year-old lieutenant, he had served on the gundeck of HMS *Swiftsure* at Trafalgar and in 1809 lost an arm in an engagement with a French frigate while serving on the HMS *Diana*. Ordered from the north Atlantic squadron to Lake Ontario in early 1813, his first command was the sloop of war HMS *Wolfe*.

Barclay's first command lasted only three weeks, until he was displaced by the arrival of Captain Sir James Yeo, appointed senior British commander on the lakes. Yeo ordered Barclay to take charge of British efforts on Lake Erie after two senior officers had turned down the command on the grounds of inadequate resources, particularly the want of seamen. Barclay proceeded to Lake Erie with three lieutenants, one surgeon, one purser, one master's mate and nineteen seamen.

Robert Heriot Barclay, commander, RN. Perry and Barclay were the same age, and both had been in their respective navies since boyhood. Barclay had been in at least two major battles prior to Lake Erie, losing an arm in 1809. He fought bravely from an inferior position and was exonerated at his court-martial in 1814. *Courtesy the John Robert Ross Collection, Toronto Public Library.*

Upon arrival at Amherstburg, he quickly understood the weakness of his position, finding the vessels only thinly manned with Canadians of the Provincial Marine. A portion of them were French Canadians who spoke no English. Barclay took command of the *Queen Charlotte* until the *Detroit* was completed on the eve of the battle. With so few men, Barclay's efforts to blockade Erie were more bluff than threat, but an effective enough bluff to impede the Americans until midsummer.

It was not until September 5 that he received reinforcements of "36 men, 2 lieutenants, 1 master's mate, and 2 gunners." These men would hardly get to know their shipmates before the battle. The total squadron muster rolls at time of the battle, as near as they can be compiled, show 572 in the British ships and 532 in the American ships. Also, one of the U.S. vessels, the schooner *Ohio*, with 12 men, was absent, having been sent back to Erie a few days before for provisions. Despite Barclay having 572 men versus Perry's 532, Perry still had an advantage in that two-thirds of his number were USN men. Barclay had the reverse ratio, with only one-third of his number RN men.

PRELIMINARIES TO BATTLE

Throughout the summer of 1813, Barclay had been intermittently blockading Erie. Periodically, weather or the need for provisions drove him off station. When Barclay withdrew from off Erie in late July, Perry could not be sure where he had gone or when he might reappear, but he moved at once to get his squadron out of the harbor. When we last left Perry, four exhausting days later, on Wednesday, August 4, with the *Lawrence* over and restowing and the *Niagara* midway through its cameling, Barclay's squadron reappeared. This was Barclay's last chance to catch the Americans at a disadvantage. With the *Lawrence*'s decks encumbered with gear and stores being carried back on board, the *Niagara* disarmed and stuck on the bar and many crewmembers of the smaller vessels scattered about in boats assisting the lightering, the squadron was desperately vulnerable. Perry would probably have suffered severe, if not catastrophic, losses from the *Queen Charlotte*'s twenty-four-pounder carronades had Barclay pressed home an attack. Such is the clarity of hindsight.

The situation looked quite different to Barclay peering through the haze of a hot summer morning at an assemblage of vessels outnumbering his own. With the wind easterly at the time, the *Lawrence* riding to a single anchor would lie head to wind, with bow pointing eastward. By coincidence, the *Niagara*, still on the bar, was pointing exactly the same way, creating the illusion that both large brigs were at anchor and able to get underway. Perry lost no time initiating a bluff. He ordered the fast schooners *Ariel* and *Scorpion* to sally out and fire a few rounds at the British. To Barclay, it looked like the whole American squadron would be after him shortly. He may have had too few men to rapidly reload for multiple broadsides.

By way of persuasion, one of the American schooners scored a lucky hit on the *Queen Charlotte*'s mizzenmast, not enough to bring it down but enough to weaken it. The brief exchanges of fire on July 21 and 22, and again on July 25 and 27, as well as this more important mini-engagement on August 4, were the only live rounds fired on Erie during the war. Barclay came about and sailed toward Long Point. As he dropped over the horizon, the balance of forces on Lake Erie tipped irretrievably in favor of the Americans. But even before Perry's ships got free of the Presque Isle bar, the American commander had demonstrated something perhaps even more important. Between July 21 and August 4, whenever he had sent his gunboats to drive off Barclay, Perry demonstrated that he was prepared to fight with whatever resources were available.

Once Perry had his ships over the bar, Barclay knew that he had lost superiority. He sailed to Long Point to land a courier and then withdrew to Amherstburg to await completion of the *Detroit*, and the arrival of hoped-for reinforcements. As undermanned as Perry's ships were, Barclay was even worse off. He had held an officer's conference, which considered sailing to and remaining at Port Dover. The advantages would be to remain close to the source of potential reinforcements and supplies while at the same time preventing Perry from getting between them and their supply line. Port Dover, however, was neither fortified nor garrisoned, and they feared that the Americans might put a landing party ashore and attack the ships moored in the river. There was also the fear that Perry would sail west and join with Harrison for an attack on Amherstburg if they left it uncovered. Barclay opted to sail to Amherstburg to protect his base and urge on the completion of the HMS *Detroit*. His ships did not venture out again until the eve of battle.

First Patrol

At 0400 in the predawn hours of August 5, Perry got underway in the *Lawrence* and sailed toward Long Point and Port Dover in pursuit of the British. Barclay had already hurried back to Amherstburg, but this was unknown to Perry. In any event, Perry's three-day cruise served as a useful shakedown for the American squadron. This sortie is also a revealing episode that may be interpreted as excessive zeal or rashness. The *Niagara* appears to have been left behind because there would not have been time to get it fitted out again after being emptied for cameling. Furthermore, Perry lacked enough officers and men to man it. On board the *Lawrence*, Perry had signed on some local militia to augment his crew, men from inland counties whom Taylor described as "never having seen water except in their own wells, and incapacitated by seasickness."

The resultant American squadron was shorthanded and untried. Crossing the bar had been an ordeal, including five days of nonstop labor with only brief snatches of rest. A more cautious commander might have rested his men and then begun a series of gradual training exercises. Perry had neither the time nor the patience for gradual steps. Very likely he felt that if he eased up at all, his exhausted crews would drop where they stood and be hard to get moving again or that morale might start to crack and that desertions could begin. The shakedown into hostile waters kept all hands on the go, with frequent drills and sailing maneuvers, including sending down topgallant masts at 0300 on the stormy second night out.

By the time they returned to anchor off Erie on the evening of Saturday, August 7, Perry and his men could not have had more than a few scattered hours of sleep in a full week of toil and danger. Yet they had begun to make the transition from a harbor-bound crowd of shipyard laborers into a seagoing fighting force. On Sunday, August 8, the squadron lay at anchor taking on stores. Perry received notice that Chauncey had finally sent significant help. Master Commandant Jesse D. Elliott, with twelve officers and ninety-one seamen, was on his way from Buffalo. Perry immediately ordered the schooner *Ariel* sent down the lakeshore to meet the party and bring it to Erie. On the next day, *Ariel* arrived late in the day with Elliott and his men. Good thing, too, for there was a storm brewing.

Perry immediately assigned Elliott to the *Niagara* and allowed him to keep the bulk of the men he had brought with him. Before Elliott's arrival, Perry had been unable to sail the *Niagara* for lack of officers and men. Now with both large brigs in capable hands, the offensive power of the squadron was effectively doubled. With this reinforcement, Perry once again did some reshuffling of assignments to best utilize his officers and spread the experience around like leavening.

There is no evidence of immediate friction between Elliott and Perry, although it is logical to suspect that Elliott may have chafed at serving under Perry. Both held the same rank of master commandant, but Perry was the senior officer in that his promotion to master commandant predated Elliott's by a few months. Against this sole factor, Elliott was senior in years (thirty-one twenty-seven), previously decorated and with greater overall

Glossary for Rig
Spars, collectively, are all the poles in the rig. Masts are vertical and on square riggers consist of (fore, main, mizzen) lower mast, topmast, topgallant mast. Yards are carried horizontally, can be set square to centerline, and take their name from the mast they are carried on. Sails bear the same name. Booms, gaffs, sprits, project out from a mast or point of attachment on the hull to spread sail on centerline. Examples: Fore Topsail is set from Fore Topsail Yard, hoisted on the Foretopmast. Fore-and-aft Mainsail (aka Spanker) is set on main gaff and boom, from the mainmast.

Standing rigging is a system of triangulation. Stays are cables tensioned leading forward on centerline, backstays a little aft on each side, which keep the masts in column. Running rigging refers to lines that control the sails.

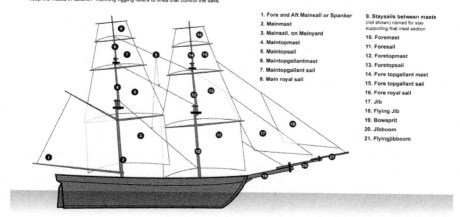

1. Fore and Aft Mainsail or Spanker
2. Mainmast
3. Mainsail, on Mainyard
4. Maintopmast
5. Maintopsail
6. Maintopgallantmast
7. Maintopgallant sail
8. Main royal sail

9. Staysails between masts (not shown) named for stay supporting that mast section
10. Foremast
11. Foresail
12. Foretopmast
13. Foretopsail
14. Fore topgallant mast
15. Fore topgallant sail
16. Fore royal sail
17. Jib
18. Flying Jib
19. Bowsprit
20. Jibboom
21. Flyingjibboom

Spar and sail plan of a large brig. A brig is two-masted, fully square-rigged on both. A fully square-rigged mast is in three sections as shown, each crossing a yard (horizontal spar) to which is bent the sail and that can be braced (angled) square to the centerline or part way to fore and aft.

command and combat experience. Elliott brought dispatches with him, including Chauncey's letter of July 30, responding to Perry's complaints of the twenty-seventh. Chauncey had received Perry's letter so quickly because he was anchored at the mouth of the Niagara River rather than at Sackets Harbor. Considering the surliness and sarcasm that Perry had expressed to his superior, including going over his head to the secretary of the navy, Chauncey's reply was remarkably restrained. Still, it clearly rebuked Perry. What has become the most famous quote from this letter reads:

> *I regret that you are not pleased with the men sent you by Messrs. Champlin and Forrest, for to my knowledge a part of them are not surpassed by any seamen we have in the fleet, and I have yet to learn that the Colour of the skin, or cut and trimmings of the coat, can effect a man's qualifications or usefulness. I have nearly 50 blacks onboard this Ship and many of them are amongst my best men.*

Later in the letter there is a quite unsubtle hint:

> *As you assured the Secretary that you conceive yourself <u>equal or superior</u> to the enemy with a force in men so much less than I had deemed necessary, there will be a great deal expected from you by your Country.*

This was a reference to the letter to the secretary, of July 20, in which Perry, lest he be thought reluctant to fight, tacked on a last sentence expressing confidence of victory no matter what the odds. As an additional zinger, Chauncey also addressed Perry's writing to the secretary, who had copied Chauncey:

> *I was mortified to see by your letters to the Secretary...that you complain...you could not get instructions from me in time...intimating the necessity of <u>Separate Command</u>—would it not have been as well to have made the same complaint to me instead of the Secretary. My confidence in your Zeal and abilities is undiminished, and I sincerely hope that your success may equal your utmost wishes.*

Chauncey had to take issue with Perry's attitude, not to mention the impropriety of going over his superior officer to complain to the secretary of the navy. Another consideration for Chauncey was that if Perry managed to make Lake Erie a separate command, Chauncey would have no claim on any prize money awarded that squadron. Yet clearly Chauncey wished to let his sensitive subordinate save face as much as possible with a conventionally polite conclusion. This last part was lost on Perry. Prone to fits of temper, with his irritability doubtless exacerbated by exhaustion, Perry sank into a fit of depression. He continued to stew in a black mood on August 10, not helped by the weather. A storm was blowing, he had to set a second anchor and his topgallant masts housed. Perry gave in to anger, and in an absolutely astonishing move, he wrote to the secretary of the navy requesting to be relieved of his command and transferred, stating that he could no longer serve under Chauncey:

> *Sir,*
>
> *I am under the disagreeable necessity of requesting a removal from this Station...I cannot serve longer under an officer who has been so regardless of my feelings...*[several paragraphs follow of point by point refutation of Chauncey's letter]*...I beg <u>most respectfully</u> and most <u>earnestly</u> that I may be immediately removed from this station.*

This must have been a case of extreme fatigue leading to a bad decision. Otherwise it is unimaginable that a patriotic, bright, ambitious, professional naval officer, in time of war, in a combat zone and in a critical command position, with action looming, would go over the head of his commanding officer and request relief because his feelings were hurt! This letter, too, would come back to haunt Perry.

THE SQUADRON SAILS WEST

By next day, the gale had blown itself out, and Perry's mood seems to have cleared with the weather. With Elliott's reinforcement and the vessels reprovisioned, the squadron sailed from Erie at 1100 on August 12, bound for the western end of Lake Erie. Light westerly winds made for a slow passage, with only 20 miles gained by sundown. Five days were needed to work the 150 miles, with frequent drills alternating with tacking the ships. This passage was the longest period the American squadron would be continuously underway during the entire campaign. The rainy afternoon of August 16 saw the squadron anchor off Cunningham's (present-day Kelly) Island, Ohio. Some excitement came when the weather cleared: a British sail was sighted fleeing toward Detroit. The *Scorpion* went in pursuit but ran aground on the shoal extending from the eastern end of Middle Bass Island. Fortunately, the wind shifted to a stiff northwesterly, which helped get it off undamaged.

Over the next four weeks, the squadron shifted anchorages frequently. From August 18 to 22, the squadron lay off Sandusky, and during this time, General Harrison arrived with several of his officers to confer with Perry. Harrison and Perry, meeting here for the first time, each liked what they saw in the other. The degree of cooperation between the army and navy in this campaign set an exemplary standard, rarely bettered before or since.

On August 25, they tacked up toward Amherstburg and observed the British squadron through telescopes. The entrance had numerous shoals and islets, all uncharted at the time, and lay under the guns of Fort Malden and a few outlying batteries. Sailing in to attack the British may have been discussed, but Perry wisely kept his distance. The Americans were not in good shape to attack, with about one-third of the squadron, including Perry, quite ill with fever and dysentery. In fact, through most of that summer, Perry's most vexing problem before the battle was the amount of sickness in the U.S. squadron. Surgeon's Mate Usher Parsons wrote:

> *After a week or ten days had elapsed, the crews were attacked with a Bilious Remittent fever, to the number of twenty or thirty per day...*

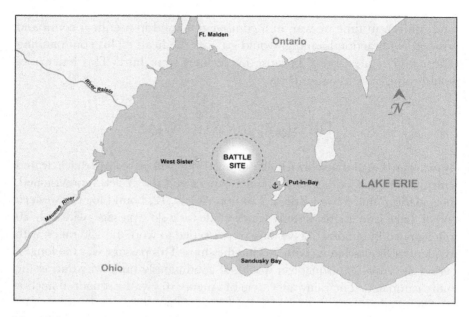

Map of the western end of Lake Erie. In the three weeks from mid-August to the time of the battle, Perry shifted anchorage several times, training his men and keeping up a blockade of the British base.

during two or three days...more than one hundred lay sick...On the day previous to the action, the number of sick in the squadron was reduced to seventy six—thirty one of whom were on board the Lawrence, *and nearly as many on board the* Niagara.

Purser Samuel Hambleton's diary records:

Our crews had been sickly, in consequence of drinking the Lake water, which gives them the Dysentery. All of the officers of our Brig, except myself, have been affected by it. Among the most seriously ill were the squadron's surgeons, all of whom were too feeble to perform their duties on the day of the battle.

Having made a reconnaissance, Perry retired to Put-in-Bay to recuperate for a few days. On Wednesday, September 1, Perry weighed anchor and sailed back to the Detroit River mouth. By noon, they were again in sight of the British base. With the weather getting squally and the sick list still large, Perry again withdrew. By next day, the squadron was again anchored off Sandusky where Perry received two letters from Secretary of the Navy William Jones, written on August 18. The first ordered the removal of Purser Magrath from command of the *Caledonia* and plainly expressed annoyance: "You have complained very much, and it appears to me very unreasonably of the want of Officers…surely you do not expect the Frigates to be stript of the Senior Lieutenants, in order to furnish you with what you are pleased to consider experienced Officers."

The same letter also criticized Perry for allowing his discontent with the quality of his crews to be known to General Harrison. Altogether it must have been face-reddening reading for Perry. In the second letter, Jones denied Perry the transfer that he had so rashly sought, but the overall tone of this denial was quite conciliatory, telling Perry that Chauncey

> has never ceased to speak of you, in terms of the highest approbation and confidence. Sensible as I am of your love of Country, high sense of honor, and zealous devotion to the service, I cannot but believe, that reflection will allay the feelings of discontent which you have expressed. The indulgence of such feelings, must terminate in the most serious injury to the service, and probably ruin to yourself. Avoid recrimination—persevere in the zealous and honourable path of duty which you have hitherto pursued with so much credit to yourself, and utility to your Country; and the result, I have not doubt, will enhance the fame of both.

The letter noted that if Perry still wanted a transfer at the end of the sailing season, it would be granted. Perry must have been greatly relieved to receive this gracious a reply to his impetuous complaints sent from Erie. Since departing Erie, Perry had written both Jones and Chauncey to inform them of his movements. Curiously, none of these letters stated a withdrawal of the request for transfer. It is hard to imagine an officer of Perry's energy and zeal, once reinforced and out on the lake in command of ten vessels and with action soon likely, doing any less than his utmost to succeed, whatever his feelings for his distant superior. Therefore, it is very surprising that he did not write, if not an apology, at least a statement requesting to retain his command. Perhaps the letter does not survive, because it is a most curious omission.

THE GREAT GUNS

"Exercised the great guns," a statement that appears with great frequency in the log of the *Lawrence* during the summer of 1813, refers to the ship's cannons, guns that were large enough to require several men to service. Delivering this concentration of artillery into battle was the focal point of the ship's mission—its very reason for existence. Maneuvering the ship with speed and precision in order to bring these guns to bear was a life-or-death business. The speed and accuracy with which they could be fired was crucial to the vessel's survival, let alone success. Frequent drills consumed a large portion of the ship's routine.

The two large brigs in the U.S. Lake Erie squadron each carried a heavy "main battery" of two twelve-pounder long guns and eighteen thirty-two-pounder carronades. Guns were designated by the weight of the balls that they fired. The long guns had a length of bore up to eighteen times the diameter of the shot they fired. Such guns were mounted on four-wheeled carriages that allowed them to be shifted to different positions on deck at need. On the *Niagara*, the long guns were mounted in the bow to fire on a fleeing enemy, hoping to score a damaging hit that would slow the prey. If being pursued by a more powerful foe, their wheeled carriages could be rolled the length of the gun deck to fire out of the stern ports in the hopes of slowing the pursuit.

The carronades (named for the foundry in Carron, Scotland, that first developed the type in 1778) were shorter, and the gun tubes were thinner-walled. Such guns were lighter for a given weight of shot and were typically mounted on sliding carriages that pivoted at the forward end. Compared to long guns, they could be served faster by a smaller crew. The catch was that carronades had a shorter range. It came down to a choice of striking power versus the range at which it could be delivered. The combined weight of a 12-pounder long gun and carriage was about 3,000 pounds. For the same weight allowance, a carronade could be mounted that threw a 32-pound ball. The trade-off was between being able to throw a 12-pound ball just over a mile or a 32-pound ball just under half a mile.

Sizing the guns to the ship was determined by a combination of factors, including the size and stability of the ship, available deck space and strength of decks. Because both rate of fire and accuracy were low, the probability of hits was increased by mounting as many guns as possible on a given length of deck. A large ship carried not just more but also heavier guns. As size increased, the weight of shot in a broadside went up disproportionately. Combined with the larger hull being the steadier gun platform and sturdier structure, all of the advantages went to the larger vessel.

Twelve-pounder long gun, named for the weight of solid round shot it fired. Its range was about one mile, or slightly over. Gun tube, carriage and fittings add up to about three thousand pounds on the deck. A well-drilled crew could manage one round per minute, at least for the first few minutes of a battle. *Photo by John Baker, courtesy Erie Maritime Museum.*

Thirty-two-pound carronade. For the same weight allowance, a carronade with sliding carriage, a proportionately shorter and thinner walled gun, could fire a thirty-two-pound ball but only out to half a mile, and really effective only below one-third of a mile. *Photo by John Baker, courtesy Erie Maritime Museum.*

A ship armed primarily with carronades could fire the maximum broadside weight for its size, but it had first to get within range. The obvious danger was that an enemy ship armed with long guns might be able to disable it before it could even fire a shot. For large vessels, the choice of dividing the battery was an obvious compromise. By the time of the War of 1812, most frigates carried long guns on the gun deck and lighter carronades on the upper, or spar, deck.

The trend on the smaller vessels was to arm primarily with carronades. Because a small vessel is more affected by wave action, it is a less steady gun platform. Even in calm conditions, smoothbore guns firing round shot had little chance of a hit at long range. The pattern emanating from the muzzles of a broadside can best be described as a "cone of improbability" as the range increases. There was still every incentive to open fire as soon as possible in the hope of getting lucky and bringing down a mast or inflicting other disabling damage early on. Most actions, however, were only decided after closing to "can't miss" range, at which point weight of shot and rapidity of fire usually determined the outcome. These factors created the incentive for smaller warships to arm predominantly with carronades.

Time and again, it was demonstrated that the best tactic for winning a battle was to fire into the enemy hull to kill and maim enough of the crew that the survivors were discouraged into surrendering. Smashing everything in its path, solid shot also sprayed a storm of wooden splinters in the process. Most casualties were the result of these splinter wounds. Sharp, jagged pieces of wood torn out of the ship's structure were the lethal equivalents of shrapnel from exploding shells. A naval battle was a close-range artillery duel between tightly packed masses of men confined within a wooden structure. As might be expected, the "butcher's bill" was often horrific.

Without tremendous discipline, the chaos in such a battle would be overwhelming. Frequent drills instilled the firing sequence so thoroughly that it would be adhered to in battle amid the distractions of choking smoke, deafening explosions, shattered wood, torn limbs, sprayed blood and screaming wounded. Concurrently, the drill developed proficiency and speed to be able to do it to them faster than they could do it to you. Everything about the guns was serious business, starting with the mere presence on board of such heavy objects. The threat of a "loose cannon" referred to a gun coming adrift in heavy weather and sliding about the deck, smashing and crushing all in its path. A truism for any gun, but especially true for naval artillery, is that "the guns are only dangerous to the enemy if you ever meet the enemy, but they are dangerous to you all of the time." There were numerous ways to make mistakes in the drill, with serious consequences. The sequence for directing this lethality had many slight variations, but a typical procedure for gun drill is found in Appendix I.

The solid round shot from cannons tended to either skip across the surface or sink deep after striking water. Thus, below-waterline hits were rare and usually the result of chance when a gust of wind combined with a trough in the waves to expose a portion of bottom planking to puncture. Normally, achieving victory amounted to winning through attrition. The fastest rate of fire for a heavy gun was perhaps one round per minute. This rate would inevitably slow as the action progressed due to fatigue, casualties among the gun crews and damage to the guns. But the endurance of a crew to stand by its gun and keep up the hot work often prevailed.

During the period of training and preparation, Perry conferred with his vessel commanders to review battle plans. Surviving order books show that Perry wrote to his vessel commanders on August 20 concerning signals and challenges to be used upon sight of a strange sail. He also sketched diagrams of a two-column cruising formation and two versions of an "Established Line of Battle."

It was at the Sandusky anchorage where Perry wrote a "General Order," issued on September 4. The "Established line of Battle" is given as *Trippe*, *Somers*, *Niagara*, *Lawrence*, *Caledonia*, *Scorpion*, *Porcupine*, *Ohio* and *Tigress*, with *Ariel* to windward. A half cable (120 yards) was given as the distance between vessels. Perry's order concludes, "Note. Commanding officers are particularly enjoined to pay attention in preserving their stations in the Line, and in all cases to keep as near the *Lawrence* as possible."

Signaling between ships relied on flag hoists. The complete naval system required a large number of flags for the letters of the alphabet, numerals and repeaters, with a signal code book to interpret various abbreviated signals for frequently used phrases. It is doubtful that this level of equipment was available to this remote squadron because Perry instituted a simplified code of signals based on only a few colored flags. This code relied as much on shifting the location of the flags to different masts or other spars as on their color and numbers.

Perry was still short of men and while at Sandusky had appealed to General Harrison for help. Harrison agreed to allow Perry to recruit volunteers from his army and militia for temporary duty on board the ships—136 came forth. Some had previous experience as boatmen or even sailors, but most would serve the role of marines as marksmen in action or filling out the gun crews. Thus reinforced, Perry shifted anchorages back to Put-in-Bay on September

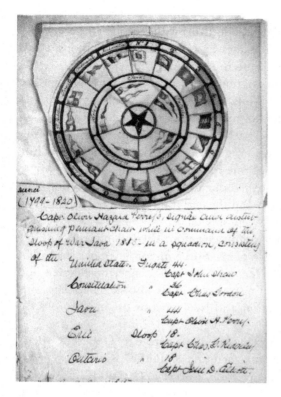

Left: Lacking the full inventory of approved equipment, Perry used a simplified code of signals, wherein a few flags could have multiple meaning depending on where in the rigging they were displayed. *Courtesy Erie Maritime Museum.*

Below: DGUTS, or "Don't Give Up the Ship," is the most iconic phrase in U.S. naval history. *Photo by John Baker, courtesy Erie Maritime Museum.*

6. Dobbins and his twelve men in the schooner *Ohio* were sent back to Erie for provisions at the time the squadron shifted anchorages. Thus, Dobbins missed the battle, not rejoining the squadron until September 14. This was the second time Perry had sent Dobbins back to Erie for resupply.

Even though the *Ohio* was armed with one twenty-four-pounder, the crew was small by naval standards, perhaps indicating that Perry thought the best use of Dobbins's local knowledge and the carrying capacity of his vessel was to have *Ohio* serve as the squadron's supply ship. Purser Samuel Hambleton's diary on September 9 notes, "Several days ago Capt. Perry convened the commanding officers in his cabin, & laid before them his plans of attacking the enemy, whenever he may appear." He also informed them of his signal for action: the motto flag already mentioned.

Perry did not know when the British would come out, but he knew that the confrontation could come at any time. These last few days before the battle were spent on various maintenance tasks, "exercising the great guns" and tending to the ever-present sick.

AMHERSTBURG, SEPTEMBER 9, 1813

Barclay was hardly prepared to come out and challenge the Americans, and he certainly wasn't driven by hubris. He had no choice. For nearly a month, the stronger American squadron had lain between him and his sources of supply, a bad situation for any military commander:

> *I should be obliged to sail with the squadron deplorably manned as it was, to fight the enemy (who blockaded the port) to enable us to get supplies of provisions and stores of every description, so perfectly destitute of provisions was the post that there was not a day's flour in store, and the crews of the squadron under my command were on half allowance of many things, and when that was done there was no more.*

The food situation was becoming critical for the whole area:

> *There were above fourteen thousand Indians to victual…To this number was to be added the whole population of that part of the country and the regular force attached to General Proctor…it was to be considered that each succeeding day added to our difficulties.*

At the time of getting underway, the situation was one of increasing privation. As Lieutenant Stokoe of the *Queen Charlotte* described it, "We might have had a week's at half allowance of provisions, but not of spirits, they were preserved for the action, and all consumed on that day, we had none served out for several days before."

Conditions must have been grim indeed to forego the grog ration! Barclay faced a stark choice. He must either fight with what he had at that moment or burn his squadron to prevent capture and watch the overextended western flank of the British position in Canada collapse—for which he would, of course, be blamed. The only hope lay in a naval victory, slim as the chance might be. With noble resignation, Barclay's squadron left its Amherstburg moorings late on September 9, dropped down the river with the current and set sail, "fully expecting to meet the enemy next morning, as they had been seen among the islands—nor was I mistaken."

Perry's most vexing problem before the battle was the sickness in the U.S. squadron. The night before the battle, 32 of 135 men on the *Lawrence* and 38 of 155 on board the *Niagara* were on the sick list, a total of 20–25 percent of all personnel. Among the most seriously ill were the squadron's surgeons, all of whom were too debilitated to perform their duties. On the day of the battle, the task of treating nearly all of the casualties devolved on one twenty-five-year-old surgeon's mate, Usher Parsons. Perry himself had been under a fever that only left him the day of the battle. Thus, the Battle of Lake Erie may be described as the day the hungry came out to fight the sick. Both sides were thoroughly miserable and in the grim mood of "let's get this over with."

THE MORNING OF THE ENGAGEMENT

SIGHTING

At daylight discovered the Enemys fleet in the NW. Made the signal immediately to the Squadron to get underway—At 6 AM the Squadron all underway working out to windward of Snake I'd to keep the weather gauge Wind at SW.

—*Sailing Master William Taylor, U.S. brig* Lawrence

The "weather gauge" meant sailing upwind of the opponent. It was the naval equivalent of the high ground in land battles. The first objective of pre-battle maneuvers in the age of sail was to secure this upwind advantage. Purser Hambleton recorded that the enemy "was visible from the deck, distant about twelve miles." It is thirty-five miles from Amherstburg to Put-in-Bay, and in the light breezes, Barclay had covered less than twenty-five miles overnight. From the deck of a ship the size of the *Lawrence*, ten or twelve miles is the limit from which one can see a sail on the horizon. At this distance, a sailing ship would look no bigger than a postage stamp seen from across a large room. The Americans had lookouts posted aloft whose view in broad daylight would have been a few miles farther, but by the time dawn had revealed the British ships, their range so close that the men who had been roused out could see them from the deck. It was very lucky for Perry that Barclay had not been able to get any closer before daylight revealed his presence.

In light air, a large naval crew could weigh (raise) anchor and set some sail in as little as fifteen minutes, although half an hour would have been

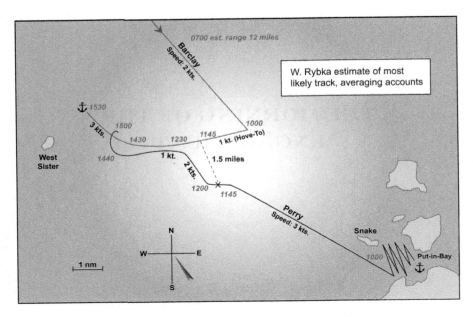

Map of the estimated track of the squadrons during the battle, based on first-person accounts.

more likely. While it may seem that Perry had ample time to get in position, the course out of the anchorage was directly into the wind. Coming from Amherstburg with a southwest breeze, Barclay enjoyed the advantage of having the wind on his beam, roughly perpendicular to the direction of travel, placing him northwest of Put-in-Bay. This gave Barclay both the weather gauge (upwind advantage) and considerable room to maneuver.

Square-rigged sailing ships have limited ability to sail into the wind. At best, they can sail to within about seventy degrees to either side of the direction the wind is coming from. The *Lawrence* and *Niagara* were particularly poor at upwind work, having been built as shallow as possible. This resulted in excessive leeway, or sideslip. Square-riggers are also at their worst in confined waters where frequent course changes are required. It takes time after each maneuver to build up speed and trim sails to best advantage, making even more leeway inevitable. Furthermore, wind tends to be deflected by islands, and it funnels directly into any channel, creating an equal headwind on either tack. And if this were not enough, the passage of the many vessels of Perry's squadron through the channel would itself scramble and impede the flow of wind to all but the lead vessels.

Perry's initial intention was to work his squadron to windward of Snake Island (now Rattlesnake Island) and get to windward of Barclay—or at least

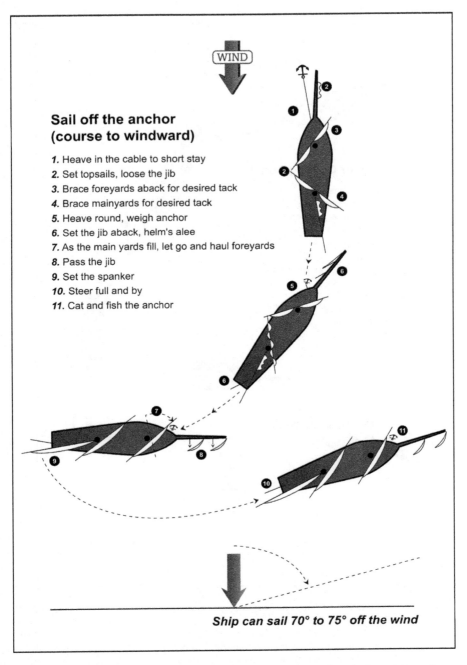

**Sail off the anchor
(course to windward)**

1. Heave in the cable to short stay
2. Set topsails, loose the jib
3. Brace foreyards aback for desired tack
4. Brace mainyards for desired tack
5. Heave round, weigh anchor
6. Set the jib aback, helm's alee
7. As the main yards fill, let go and haul foreyards
8. Pass the jib
9. Set the spanker
10. Steer full and by
11. Cat and fish the anchor

Ship can sail 70° to 75° off the wind

Sailing off the anchor. When the ship had to be got underway and worked to windward immediately because of the near proximity of land behind it, there was no room for error.

Tacking, or Coming About

1. Standby to come about
2. Ease down the helm
3. Haul the spanker to weather
4. Ease headsheets
5. Rise fore tacks and sheets
6. Mainsail haul
7. Shift the helm (only needed if she starts sternway)
8. Trice up the spanker
9. Let go and haul
10. Pass fore and aft
11. Set the foresail
12. Steer full and by

WIND

Sailing ships could not sail straight to windward, the direction the wind is coming from, but had to "fall off" to one side of the wind until the sails could fill with wind and transmit power to the hull. Tacking, or coming about, is turning the ship into the wind, during which time the vessel is counting on conserved momentum. Speed bleeds off rapidly as the sails lose their drive and, for a time, are working to push it backwards. Finally, all must be shifted over and trimmed (adjusted) to sail with the wind now on the other side. Nearly every line in the ship must be handled and every action taken at just the right time.

be clear of the harbor. This would have allowed him to form a battle line to engage on reciprocal courses with a beam wind. During this time, Perry's ships were gaining barely a few hundred feet to windward on each tack. Each tack required hauling the yards from one side to the other and passing fore-and-aft sails, and almost every line of the running rigging would need to be cleared for running or manned for hauling every few minutes. After nearly four hours and a score of tacks, Perry's ships were still not clear of the island obstructions. The situation must have been as frustrating as it was exhausting. Finally, Perry could stand it no longer, according to Sailing Master William Taylor: "The Commodore then said he would wear ship and go to leeward of the islands, as he was determined to bring the enemy to battle that day, even if he gave them the weather gauge."

When Perry ordered the wear (changing tacks by turning away from the wind), as Taylor pointed out, he was ceding the weather gauge (advantage) to the British. Perry replied that "to windward or to leeward I shall fight them this day." This statement sounds like evidence of Perry's impetuosity, but in this case there was more to it than impatience. Unless Perry could get his squadron clear of the islands before the British were upon him, he would be at an even more disastrous disadvantage, trapped with shoal waters and islands behind him. While Perry had been forced to tack repeatedly, Barclay had been able to hold his course with a fair wind.

After nearly four hours of a light but steady breeze, Barclay was getting dangerously close. Perry had to form a line somehow or risk getting caught with his ships masking one another's fire. This can be inferred from Barclay's report: "I bore up for them in hopes of bringing them to action among the islands." For Barclay to "bear up" (turn downwind) meant that he was far enough to windward, and close enough to Perry, to judge it worthwhile to turn downwind in order to trap Perry so that he could not form a line of battle. Just at the moment Barclay was about to exercise his advantage and Perry was accepting that he had to fight from a bad position, everything changed. Barclay's next words were, "[B]ut that intention was soon frustrated by the wind suddenly shifting to the south east, which brought the enemy directly to windward."

The wind shift suddenly and completely turned the tables. The U.S. vessels that had been struggling to sail to windward no longer had to do so. It was their turn to "bear up" and fall off the wind to reach the British. The fortuitous wind shift saved Perry from a very bad tactical situation. Had it not come when it did, Perry would not only have been in the disadvantaged downwind position (lee gauge), but he would also have been perilously close

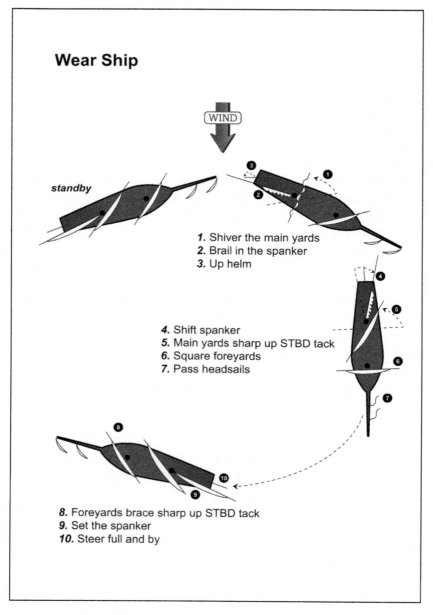

Wear Ship

standby

1. Shiver the main yards
2. Brail in the spanker
3. Up helm

4. Shift spanker
5. Main yards sharp up STBD tack
6. Square foreyards
7. Pass headsails

8. Foreyards brace sharp up STBD tack
9. Set the spanker
10. Steer full and by

Wearing ship has the same objective as tacking, to get the ship sailing with the wind on the other side. Tacking turns into the wind; wearing turns away from the wind. Wearing is used to change tacks when winds are too light to carry its momentum through or when winds are high and seas are so rough that it will lose speed and start backing down before getting across the eye of the wind.

to the rocky shoals on the northwest side of Middle and North Bass Islands. If pinned there, he would not have been able to run, nor would his large brigs have been able to get to windward and close in enough on the British to make best use of his heavy firepower advantage in carronades. Perry did, however, have superiority in heavy long guns on the smaller gunboats, so even if forced to anchor to keep off the shoals, the American squadron would have remained formidable as long as the vessels remained in a compact enough line to be mutually supporting.

CLOSING ON THE BRITISH

Though the wind direction had shifted, it remained light. The wind shift that had filled Perry's sails from astern had thrown Barclay's sails aback, forcing him to turn away from the wind to regain control. Since Barclay had been heading southeast, on starboard tack, with the wind abeam, the effect of a wind shift was to push his ships to the west, onto the larboard (port) tack. This was the better option for Barclay in any case. Had he chosen to turn east on a starboard tack, he would have been running into the same islands and shoals that were threatening Perry's ships. To the west, he had thirty miles of sea room to the Michigan shore, as well as a chance of falling back on Amherstburg if the battle did not go well.

On this westerly heading, Barclay hove-to to await Perry, keeping only enough headway to maintain steerage and a compact battle line. The British ships moving slowly away from the Americans reduced the net speed of the overtaking U.S. squadron to a walking pace, making for an agonizingly slow chase. The next hour and three quarters saw the two squadrons close to within range of long guns. During this time, the wind veered south. This can be deduced from two facts, first that Barclay hove-to so as to maintain a compact battle line, and secondly, the position given by Taylor's log at the end of the battle. Lying hove-to, the British ships would have had the wind almost on the beam. The track of a vessel in this configuration is a combination of slight headway and considerably greater leeway. Knowing the maneuver configuration, and where the ships ended up, reveals that the wind could not have stayed at southeast for long after Perry cleared the anchorage.

All accounts stress the light breezes that day. James Fenimore Cooper, who was not present but later researched the day and interviewed participants, wrote of a "two knot breeze," meaning just enough wind for the ship to make two knots of hull speed. Daniel Dobbins, also not present but later party to many discussions among the veterans, described a "three knot breeze." A

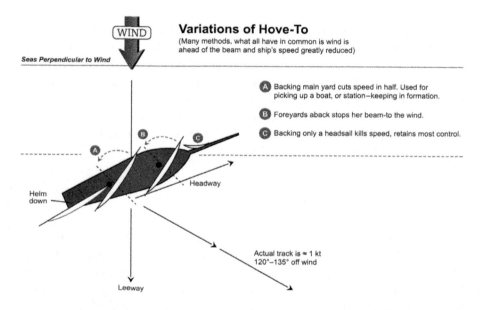

Variations of hove-to. This derives from heaving in tight on the sails so that the vessel comes up to the wind, riding with the wind forward of the beam and greatly slowed down.

rough rule of thumb for sailing warships is that at the lower end of the wind scale, vessel speed is about half of the wind speed. To sail at two or three knots requires four to six knots of wind, which would barely have ruffled the surface of the water.

DEPLOYMENT

Until the wind shift, Barclay's line would have appeared to Perry as an end-on column, preventing him from learning the identity of the individual ships. Once Barclay tacked, Perry could clearly see his order of battle, and it was not what he had expected. Perry imagined that Barclay would follow the conventional practice of placing his own flagship, the *Detroit*, in the center of the line. Instead, to take advantage of the greater range of the *Detroit*'s long guns, Barclay had placed it ahead of the *Queen Charlotte*, which was primarily armed with short-range carronades. Since Perry had expected the *Detroit* to be in the middle position, the *Niagara* was initially stationed ahead of the *Lawrence*. Perry quickly ordered Elliott to heave-to so the *Lawrence* could range alongside to permit a conference including Lieutenant Brevoort, in command of *Niagara*'s

The Morning of the Engagement

Niagara firing a gun, sailing in the same type of nearly calm condition in which the Battle of Lake Erie was fought. Note the amount of smoke from a single half-sized saluting charge (two pounds of powder) and imagine a full broadside (forty pounds of powder). *Photo by Robert Lowry, courtesy Erie Maritime Museum.*

marines. Brevoort had been on Lake Erie before the war in command of the transport schooner *John Adams* and knew the British ships by sight.

After the British ships had been identified, Perry altered his line to conform with his earlier orders regarding designated adversaries. *Niagara* was to drop astern of *Lawrence* since *Queen Charlotte* was astern of *Detroit.* The deployment of the two opposing battle lines as the squadrons drew in range was (for the United States) *Scorpion, Ariel, Lawrence, Caledonia, Niagara, Porcupine, Somers, Trippe* and *Tigress* and (for the British) *Chippewa, Detroit, Hunter, Queen Charlotte, Lady Prevost* and *Little Belt.*

During the ninety minutes between the wind shift and the opening shots, on *Lawrence* and *Niagara,* sail was reduced from "full sail," which had been used to beat to windward out of the anchorage, to "easy sail" (topsails and some fore and aft). Despite being in pursuit of Barclay, the large brigs reduced sail because Perry's vessels had widely differing sailing speeds. Large vessels are generally faster than small ones (usually in proportion to waterline length). Just as important in the light air conditions of the day was the greater height of rig on the larger vessels. The wind is usually stronger aloft, and a taller rig will catch more of it.

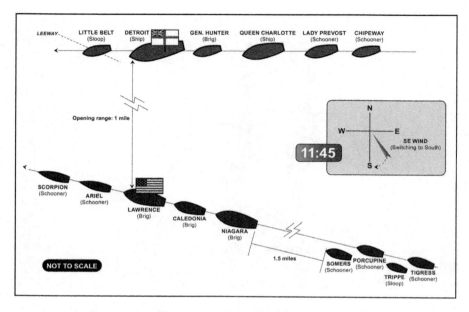

Battle of Lake Erie, opening shots. Perry has the larger squadron and outguns the British three to two in weight of shot, but many of his long guns are on the miserably slow gunboats and not in range.

The two schooners at the head of the line, *Ariel* and *Scorpion*, were the pair that Chauncey and Eckford had ordered lengthened by ten feet and that Brown had built on a sharp-hulled pilot boat model. Though smaller than the large brigs, these two had ample speed to keep up. Of the gunboats at the rear, *Porcupine* and *Tigress* were the smallest and were heavily loaded to bear thirty-two-pounder long guns. *Somers* and *Trippe* were converted merchant vessels with fuller hull forms designed for maximum cargo capacity rather than speed. In the middle of the squadron, the *Caledonia* was also a converted merchant vessel and was slower than the flagship but at least was able to keep in range. Perry kept *Lawrence* and *Niagara* under reduced sail to help the smaller vessels keep up, but it wasn't enough. As the chase wore on, the four gunboats at the rear fell ever farther behind.

During this time, the guns would have been carefully loaded and all other battle preparations made. Yard slings were doubled to lessen the chances of one of the heavy yards dropping out of the rig and onto the deck. The boats were all launched and towed either on the disengaged side or astern to prevent them becoming a source of splinter damage. Shot racks were filled adjacent to the guns, gun tools laid handy, water buckets filled for sponging the guns or dousing a fire and likewise wet blankets hung around the powder magazine. Linstocks and slow matches were readied for firing the guns, the galley fire drawn and doused, the wardroom prepared for use as a surgery room and decks sanded to give traction when the blood flowed.

With all this done, there was time to serve a cold meal of salted pork and hardtack, accompanied by the customary before-action "grog" (which in this case would most likely have been frontier rye whisky, a stiff four ounces diluted with about as much water). Perry showed his motto flag, "Don't Give Up the Ship," to his men and had it hoisted, eliciting a cheer. He then went around the deck, relieving the tension with a few words to each of the gun crews. Most, including Perry, had never been in battle. Perry had been under fire from canister and musket shot while assisting the amphibious landing near Fort George in May, but this was to be his only experience going up against the massed broadsides of enemy warships. An exception to this innocence was a small contingent that had served in *Constitution* in its victories against the *Guerriere* and *Java* the preceding year. As recalled in Purser Hambleton's diary, Perry simply said, "You fellows know just what to do."

According to Surgeon's Mate Usher Parsons, "Every preparation being made, and every man at his post, a profound silence reigned for more than one hour—the most trying part of the whole scene. It was like the stillness of the atmosphere that precedes the hurricane."

Seaman David Bunnell wrote, "This was the time to try the stoutest heart. My pulse beat quick—all nature seemed wrapped in awful suspense—the dart of death hung as it were trembling by a single hair, and no one knew on whose head it would fall."

A sailing vessel ghosting along in these conditions is indeed silent. At speeds of two to three knots, there is only the faintest rippling noise of water at the stem and at the rudder chains. There is no sigh of wind in the rigging. Running before the wind, commands from aft echo off the sails, making voices jarringly loud and encouraging conversation in whispers. On board the British ships, the mirror image of silent dread and resolve took place, until the *Detroit's* band struck up "Rule Britannia!" immediately before the firing started.

SHOTS RING OUT

The Opening Salvo

At a quarter before twelve I commenced the Action by firing a few long guns.
                                                    —Commander R.H. Barclay, RN

At ¼ before mer'n [meridian; noon] *the Enemy commenced the action at about one mile dist.—ordered the Scorpion who was on our weather to fire on the enemy.*

                                        —Sailing Master W.V. Taylor, USN

The opening round from the *Detroit*, a twenty-four-pound ball, splashed short. The *Scorpion* returned fire first because its long thirty-two-pounder outranged both the twelve-pounder long guns and the thirty-two-pounder carronades on board the *Lawrence*. A few minutes later, a second ball from the *Detroit* crashed through the *Lawrence's* bulwarks and killed a man. With his own guns mostly out of range and limited support from the long guns on board the *Scorpion* and *Ariel*, Perry sailed on for ten more minutes on a converging course to close the range before firing a twelve-pounder long gun from the *Lawrence*. Since the majority of the *Detroit's* guns were long guns, while the *Lawrence's* battery was nearly all carronades, Perry was initially far outranged and taking casualties without being able to return effective fire. He wrote:

At 15 minutes before twelve, the Enemy commenced firing; at 5 minutes before twelve, the action commenced on our part. Finding their fire very destructive,

> *owing to their long guns, and its being mostly directed at the* Lawrence, *I made sail, and directed the other vessels to follow, for the purpose of closing with the Enemy. Every brace and bowline being soon shot away, she became unmanageable, notwithstanding the great exertions of the Sailing Master.*

The total number of guns mounted was sixty-three British to fifty-four American, but many of the British guns were mere 4- or 6-pounders. In broadside weight of carronades, the Americans outgunned the British 492 pounds to 320. In long guns, even if only counting 9-pounders and up, the Americans mounted seventeen guns to the British fifteen, with a throw weight disparity of 288 pounds to 183. Overall, the Americans significantly outgunned the British in both long guns and carronades.

Perry's immediate problem was the uneven distribution of his firepower. The majority of the long guns, and all of the heaviest (twenty-four- and thirty-two-pounders), were mounted in the small gunboats: the *Ariel*, *Scorpion* and *Caledonia* near the *Lawrence* and the *Somers*, *Porcupine*, *Tigress* and *Trippe* in the rear. In the long chase preceding the battle, the four slower vessels had lagged behind and were now far out of range. It was only in the ship-to-ship duel of the *Detroit* versus the *Lawrence* that the British had a marked superiority in long guns, but that individual duel might now decide the entire battle. The *Lawrence*, outranged by and suffering hits from *Detroit*'s long guns, was converging at an agonizingly slow rate in a dying breeze. Since maintaining course invited disaster, Perry needed to make a decision between two options: one, set more sail and alter course to close the range as rapidly as possible, or two, "haul his wind" (alter course toward the wind) to open the range, tack back to reform his squadron and then concentrate his own long gun fire.

There was still half the day left, and Perry held the weather gauge with nine vessels to six and a three-to-two advantage in weight of shot, even if some of it was lagging far astern. The conservative approach would have been to break off the engagement, close up his squadron and try later in the day to attack with a better concentration of force. Instead, Perry chose to accept an extreme level of risk and immediately close the range, regardless of the punishment that his ships and men would suffer on the way in. He ordered more sail and a turn to starboard, determined at all costs to close with the British line.

Although it is impossible to re-create Perry's decision process with certainty, it is likely that at the center of it all was a realization of the timeliness of that moment. For many months, all of his energy had been ceaselessly focused

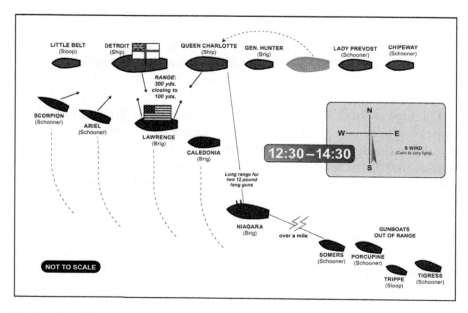

Battle of Lake Erie, closing. Perry accepts the extreme risk of sailing bows on toward the enemy, enduring raking fire until at extremely close range. For the next two hours, the ships were nearly becalmed. The failure of Elliott in the *Niagara* to closely support Perry allowed the British to concentrate fire on the *Lawrence*, resulting in horrific casualties.

on reaching this point. The long, hard, improbable winter spent gathering men, ships and guns on the frozen lakeshore; the fervent and ambiguous exchanges of letters with his superiors, too easily ascribed to idle bluster or timidity; and the razor-sharp dueling personalities of his junior officers, all alert to their brother's courage and fitness—all of these factors now rested on the shoulders of this young officer and were about to be crystallized by one decision: either further delay or decisive action. Through a more cautious response and a studied regathering of his forces, the moment that he had created would be lost.

An added weight on Perry's mind, pushing him toward the riskiest option, was the nagging memory of the rash request for transfer he had sent to the secretary of the navy. Now that he was under fire and men had been hit, if Perry hauled out of range to regroup his squadron and Barclay somehow got away (which with an obviously smaller squadron he had some incentive to attempt), it might appear that it was Perry who was avoiding action. Coupled with his request for transfer, some might infer that he wasn't up to the burden of command or, worst of all, might cast doubt on his courage.

The hot-tempered letters sent by Perry were now creating a self-imposed pressure to accept grave risk and the need to demonstrate his courage and zeal by engaging at the first opportunity.

The immediate and dreadful risk that Perry took by this change in course was in exposing his vessels to raking fire while closing the range. With his bow pointed at the British line, his broadside guns were unable to bear—while each British broadside tore the length of the *Lawrence*'s deck, scything through the clustered gun crews from one end of the ship to the other. Through this ordeal there lurked the even greater risk that the breeze would die out altogether and leave the *Lawrence* dead in the water before achieving carronade range. If that had happened, the Americans would have been shot to bloody splinters with no very effective way to return fire. The one hope then would have been to use the sweeps to close the range. Speed under sweeps was at best two knots, and the time exposed to raking fire might have been fatally prolonged.

The *Lawrence* set more sail, the topgallants and royals. Several times Perry ordered the helm to sharply swing broadside and fire a few carronades, the first lieutenant spotting from the bow to see if they were yet in range. The shots being spotted by the first lieutenant required turning the ship from running downwind to nearly across the wind in order to bring the guns to bear and slow the closing. As soon as hits were observed, the entire broadside was loosed. While reloading, Perry pressed on to get to the short range at which his carronades would be most lethal.

CLOSE ACTION

At ½ past Mer'n within musket shot of the Enemy's new ship Detroit. *At this time they opened a most destructive fire on the* Lawrence—*from their whole squadron. Continu'd to near them as fast as possible.*
—*Sailing Master Taylor*

As Perry ordered the *Lawrence* through raking fire into the midst of the British squadron, he expected the rest of his squadron to follow him in. The *Ariel* and *Scorpion* kept station toward the head of the British line, and the slow *Caledonia* endeavored to close as well. The *Niagara*, however, did not. At the moment the helm was put up on the *Lawrence* and held steady on the *Niagara*, a bitter and never-resolved controversy began between Perry and Elliott. The heart of the dispute is whether Elliott's failure to closely follow Perry was the result of a deliberate and implicitly cowardly decision or due to the vagary of the wind that left him unable to follow.

According to Usher Parsons:

> *The* Niagara *did not make sail with the* Lawrence *and accompany her down into close action as ordered, but continued her long shot with two bow guns…The* Caledonia *astern followed the* Lawrence *into close action against her antagonist the* Hunter. *But the* Niagara, *which when the battle began was within hail of the* Lawrence, *did not follow her down toward the enemy's line, so as to encounter her antagonist the* Queen Charlotte.

On board the *Lawrence*, Parsons cared for all of the wounded of both squadrons after the battle and, thus, probably conversed with more of the participants than any other individual. While his sense of overall events may have been complete, he was not actually an eyewitness to the battle after the shooting started. His station was down below in the wardroom (officer's dining room), which on small warships customarily became the surgeon's operating room during battle. However, according to Usher Parsons:

> *The wounded began to come down before the* Lawrence *opened her battery…it seemed as though heaven and earth were at loggerheads. For more than two long hours, little could be heard but the deafening thunders of our own broadsides, the crash of balls dashing through our timbers, and the shrieks of the wounded. These were brought down faster than I could attend to them, farther than to stay the bleeding, or support the shattered limbs with splints, and pass them forward upon the berth deck.*

The waterlines of the *Lawrence* and *Niagara* would have been at about knee level for men standing in the wardroom, or anywhere else on the berth deck. Since the sides of the ship could be readily pierced by solid shot, those below deck were still exposed to lethal fire. During the battle, no fewer than five balls crashed through the small wardroom surgery—in two cases dismembering and putting an end to the agony of the wounded men on whom Parsons was operating. A consequence of the ships having been built to shoal draft requirements was that the handling room of the powder magazine could not be gotten below the waterline. Powder barrels could be low enough in the bilge to avoid a hit, but the gunner and his assistants stood exposed while ladling charges into flannel bags. These bags were passed to the powder monkeys through a slit in a wet blanket hung as a spark screen.

While at this work, a British ball shattered the lamp-room lantern and window through which the magazine was illuminated. As remembered by Taylor in a letter, the candle fell out of the lantern and, still lit, plunged toward an open powder cask. A quick catch in the open palm of a gunner put the candle out and saved the ship from oblivion. No matter the level of courage, skill and determination put forth, survival in such situations is very often pure chance.

One measure of the ferocity of the battle is a complaint voiced by the wounded that "blood was dripping upon us through the plank seams of the gun deck above." One of the wounded near the end of the battle was Purser Hambleton. A large splinter torn from one of the spars pierced his shoulder from above, and he was many months recovering. His diary records:

> The Caledonia, *Lieut. Turner, was close astern of us*—the Ariel, *Lieut. Packet,* & Scorpion, *Sailing Master Champlin were on our larboard bow—and these 4 vessels sustained the fire of the enemy almost exclusively for more than two hours in which time we had twenty two men killed and sixty one wounded. The ship was a complete wreck the rigging cut to pieces—masts and spars wounded & almost every gun on the starboard side dismounted or in some way disabled…The* Niagara, *all this time, was a long way astern of the* Caledonia & *the Gunboats* Somers, Trippe, Tigress & Porcupine *considerable distance in line, astern of her. It is the general opinion of the officers that, during the time I spoke of, we did not receive the least support from them.*

The British view of this period of the action agrees. Again quoting Barclay's report to Yeo:

> About a quarter past the American Commodore…came to close action with the Detroit, *the other Brig of the Enemy apparently destined to engage the* Queen Charlotte…*kept so far to Windward as to render the* Queen Charlotte's *24 pr Carronades useless.*

Barclay's statement is clear: the *Niagara* remained out of carronade range. He also mentions the fire of the gunboats astern, as well as from the *Caledonia*. The American gunboats lagging behind had only one gun each, but these were thirty-two-pounder long guns, the most powerful in service at the time. They were at the outside limit of their range but might have scored an occasional hit. Small gunboats were usually ineffective warships. They were not very seaworthy, and due to their limited size, it would take very little wave action to make them wildly inaccurate gun platforms. The nearly calm conditions of that day were one of the rare instances under which their fire could be effective when they finally crawled into range. An affidavit written in 1818 by Sailing Master Champlin (commanding officer of *Scorpion*) noted, "The *Queen Charlotte* made sail & closed up with the *Detroit*, shortly after the action commenced, and directed her fire at the *Lawrence*. The *Niagara* still continued to remain a long way astern and firing at long shot."

There is no doubt that Elliott lagged behind during the height of the battle. Elliott could be said to have been continuously engaged as long as his twelve-pounders were in range, but closely engaged would have required closing to within carronade range. Why Elliott stood off for so long has been in dispute ever since that day. His obvious defense was lack of wind. In sultry and light air conditions, there are often "holes" in the wind, patches of dead calm in between areas of light breeze. The persistence of this calm spot affecting only the *Niagara* is less credible. The *Queen Charlotte* was downwind of *Niagara* and had enough wind to pass the *Hunter* and closely support the *Detroit*. The slow-sailing *Caledonia* just ahead of *Niagara* was able to close, although its commander, Lieutenant Daniel Turner, wisely kept just out of range of British carronades but well within range of his own guns, which were a pair of twenty-four-pounder long guns.

If the *Niagara*'s pair of twelve-pounder long guns were used throughout the action, then its distance from the British line could not have been much over a mile. Getting within carronade range meant closing to just under half a mile. Reaching effective range meant closing another quarter mile. To cover three quarters of a mile in less than two hours does not require much speed. In the light air at the beginning of the battle, the *Lawrence* covered the same distance in half an hour. Elliott's defenders have also made much of his being constrained, in the absence of further signals from Perry, by the order to maintain his station in line and that he was thus held back by the slow-sailing *Caledonia*.

Perry's order was in three parts: engage your designated adversary, stay close to the *Lawrence* and stay in line. When circumstances render it impossible to do all three, clinging to the least important, to the exclusion of the other two, is hard to justify. The argument that even if Elliott misjudged his priorities it was up to Perry to command him to do otherwise via signaling is logical but naïve given the practical difficulty of communicating by flag in such light air that flags hung limp and smoke from the guns hung in dense clouds.

Between 12:30 p.m. and 2:30 pm, the static relative positions of the ships indicate that the breeze died to a flat calm. This can be inferred from

Use of sweeps. On several occasions, the present-day *Niagara* has demonstrated that even untrained rowers can move it along at 1.5 to 2.0 knots. *Photo by Linda Bolla.*

Perry's statement that the *Lawrence* was "becoming unmanageable" and yet maintained a static position relative to the British ships. It would seem that having missed the chance earlier, Elliott was now stuck in position, unable to close regardless of what sails were set. This defense ignores the option of using the sweeps. Even if the wind had gone flat calm, Elliott should have had recourse to the sweeps. The *Niagara* was definitely built with sweep ports, as is known from the wreck that came up in 1913. In March, Dobbins had paid for taking delivery of sixty sweeps, twenty to twenty-five feet long, and eighteen sweeps would have been a full inventory. The present *Niagara* has been maneuvered at over two knots by sweeps. Even at a mere one knot, Elliot could have closed the range in a half to three quarters of an hour. It cannot be proved with certainty that *Niagara* had its sweeps on board, but the

89

ship being built to have them and Dobbins taking delivery of an adequate number to outfit the vessels is strong circumstantial evidence that Elliott had it within his power to close the range, even in a flat calm.

Elliott had been under fire before and had acquitted himself well, so it is too simplistic to write him off as a coward. There is also no evidence to indicate traitorous intent. Instead, the evidence points to an insubordinate officer who deemed that he knew better than his commander. Elliott, encouraged by Magrath, judged Perry to be making a catastrophic error and perhaps decided not to fall into the same trap. Yet however risky and ill-considered was Perry's decision to close, the wind did hold *just* long enough for the *Lawrence* to get into close range. If Elliott had followed Perry as ordered, the fire superiority of the Americans would have been decisive and the battle would have been over in half the time and with far fewer casualties. Everyone who was there knew it, including Elliott. Ever since, his defenders have either been drawn from among uncomfortable subordinates dependent on Elliott's recommendation for promotion or from those familiar with his good qualities but who had not witnessed the battle and the terrible punishment taken by the *Lawrence* and those on board it.

According to Sailing Master Taylor:

> *At ½ past 1 pm so entirely disabled that we could work the Brig no longer called the Men from the Tops & Marines to man the guns—at this time our braces—bowlines—sheets & just almost every strand of rigging cut off—Masts & spars cut through in various places—At 2 pm most of the guns dismounted breechings gun carriages knocked to pieces—called the few surviving men from the first division to man the guns aft.*

The fact that the masts stood with serious damage and all the supporting rigging severed is further evidence the wind had died altogether. Also, if the *Lawrence* was so badly shot up aloft, the reason it stayed in continuous close action with the *Detroit* and *Queen Charlotte* was that none of these vessels could move under sail at this time.

There is a truly amazing story of courage and unit cohesion here, perhaps equaled but never surpassed in the annals of the U.S. Navy. Understanding this heart-pounding drama is ironically enhanced by some dry statistics. There is a remarkable consistency in the casualty figures of all the naval engagements of the War of 1812. The ratio of killed to wounded averaged about one to four. The combined total casualties were between 12 percent and 15 percent for the victor and about 30 percent on board the vanquished.

Sinking of ships, and attendant loss of most of the crew to drowning, was a rare occurrence. Solid shot striking water either skipped high or lost velocity and plunged. Hits at the waterline resulting in flooding were rare. The object was to capture the enemy vessel, which might have valuable cargo on board or could be repaired for use by the victor. The surest means of accomplishing capture was closing the range and firing into the opposing crew. The race was to be first to kill and maim enough of the men to discourage the rest into surrender. When the "butcher's bill" got to the point where one out of three men were bleeding and the ability to return fire was rapidly diminishing as fewer were able to work the guns, the situation became hopeless. A demoralized crew would cry for "quarter," and the surviving officers, generally recognizing the futility of taking further casualties, hauled down their flag.

Something very different took place on board the *Lawrence*. By 2:30 p.m., there were 22 dead and 61 wounded from a complement of 103 "effectives," a staggering 80 percent. Actually, a portion of those on the sick list roused themselves to fight, so the number of men engaged was a little higher and the percentage of loss slightly lower, but the results were catastrophic by any measure. Yet this crew did not break. Clearly, Perry displayed a most charismatic and determined leadership to inspire this level of courage from his men. They fought until their ship was helpless and still did not give up. It would have seemed that Perry was facing certain defeat. His ship could no longer maneuver or fight and had suffered horrific casualties, but at this seemingly impossible minute, the wind once again saved him.

PERRY'S TRANSFER TO THE *NIAGARA*

In this situation, she [the Lawrence] sustained the action upwards of two hours, within canister distance, until every gun was rendered useless, and the greater part of her crew either killed or wounded. Finding she could no longer annoy the Enemy, I left her in charge of Lt. Yarnall...At half past two, the wind springing up, Capt. Elliott was enabled to bring his vessel, the Niagara, *gallantly into close action. I immediately went on board of her.*

—O.H. Perry

The Action continued with great fury until half past two, when I perceived my opponent to drop astern and a Boat passing from him to the Niagara *(which Vessel was at this time perfectly fresh).*

—R.H. Barclay

Two phrases imply the windless calm just before this time: Perry's "the wind springing up" and Barclay's "I perceived my opponent to drop astern." The *Lawrence* dropped astern because it was the most heavily damaged aloft and therefore affected less by the rising wind. Dropping back was in relative motion as the other ships were being carried forward at a faster rate. Yarnall and Taylor waited until Perry arrived on board *Niagara* before lowering the *Lawrence*'s ensign to avoid taking further casualties with the ship helpless.

What was the *Niagara*'s position at the time of Perry's transfer? From the viewpoint at the head of the line, Sailing Master Stephen Champlin, commander of the *Scorpion,* observed:

> *A short time before Comd're Perry's going onboard of her she ranged ahead of the* Lawrence *and to windward: bringing the Comdr's ship between her and the enemy; where she might have passed to leeward and relieved the* Lawrence *from their destructive fire: the wind being at that time S.E. and the American squadron steering large (with the exception of the* Lawrence, *she being at that time entirely disabled and lying like a log upon the water).*

Early in the battle, Barclay suffered a splinter wound to his thigh, got it bandaged and returned to the deck. Now he was wounded again, this time seriously. His right shoulder blade was smashed by a grapeshot ball. He had lost his left arm in action against the French years earlier, and now this injury rendered him truly helpless. The severity of this wound probably saved his life, as he could no longer keep the deck and was carried below, sparing him further exposure to heavy fire, which was about to increase markedly. Grape is short-range ammunition, carrying only three hundred yards at most, and its presence at this point in the battle indicates that Elliott and the *Niagara* had finally become closely engaged. Other reports corroborate that *Niagara* was firing full broadsides before Perry's boarding.

With Barclay seriously wounded, command of the *Detroit* devolved on Second Lieutenant George Inglis (First Lieutenant John Garland had been mortally wounded earlier). In his subsequent report to Barclay, Inglis stated that "after your being wounded the Enemy's second Brig, at that time on our weather beam, shortly after took a position on our weather bow, to rake us."

Two statements from the 1815 inquiry are of interest here. *Niagara*'s sailing master Nelson Webster testified that "after we got into close action I was knocked down and carried below, when I came on deck again Capt. Perry was onboard." *Niagara* midshipman John Montgomery testified, "When

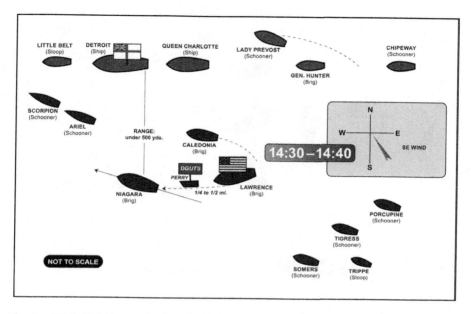

Battle of Lake Erie, just at the time the last gun is silenced on board the *Lawrence*, the wind springs up and saves Perry. Determined to gain the day, he transfers by boat to the *Niagara*.

Com. Perry came onboard we were firing all our starboard guns…we had kept up an increased fire from our carronades some time before Com. Perry came onboard."

Taken together, these statements point to the *Niagara* having been close enough to the *Detroit* for at least one broadside of grapeshot, which would later allow Elliott to claim that he had been closely engaged before Perry's transfer, even if only for a few minutes. Later in the inquiry, Montgomery described the sail handling at that time: "We took a position which brought the *Lawrence* nearly astern of us on the lee quarter. Captain Elliott ordered us to make sail, and we had boarded the fore tack and were in the act of setting topgallant sails, before Capt. Perry came on board."

Apparently, Elliott was sailing for the head of the British line with the intention of taking a raking position. Setting more sail increased both his speed and the distance that Perry's cutter had to row to reach the *Niagara*. The British recognized the significance of the boat departing the *Lawrence* and shifted fire to it. All in the boat were soaked by the splash of nearby misses. If Perry had been hit and not made it to the *Niagara*, his name might be only a small, sad footnote about a rash and inexperienced young commander who

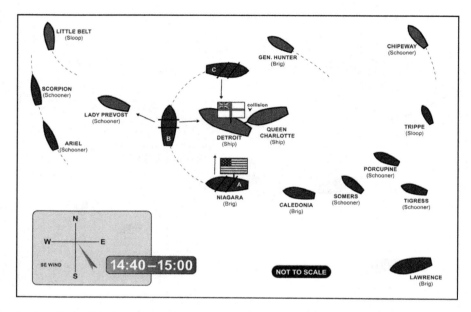

Battle of Lake Erie, breaking the British line. Perry sails the *Niagara* across the bows of the badly damaged British ships. Double-shotted broadsides soon force the British to surrender. In the space of half an hour, Perry has gone from catastrophic defeat to a total victory.

died in futility after abandoning his men and fleeing his ship in defeat, while clutching a banner proclaiming "Don't Give Up the Ship!" In his place there would now be the name of Elliott on all of the statues, in Elliott Squares, in Elliotvilles and in Elliott Counties all over Ohio, Pennsylvania and New York. It appears that despite all his delay and previous hesitation, Elliott would have done what Perry was about to do.

Not surprisingly, there is no agreement about what exactly was said between Perry and Elliott when they met on board the *Niagara* that day. Perry's report to Secretary Jones describes Elliott's next action: "[W]hen he anticipated my wishes, by volunteering to bring the schooners, which had been kept astern by the lightness of the wind, into closer action." Whether he volunteered or was sent, Elliott took the cutter that had brought Perry and was rowed back to the lagging gunboats, boarding the *Somers*. It was a superfluous errand—with the rising wind, these vessels were closing up in any case. This southeast wind, in fact, would have reached these gunboats first, allowing them to close the range before the wind reached the heavily engaged vessels. The gunboats were close enough to be firing grape by the end of the battle, which was only minutes away.

Victory

According to Commodore O.H. Perry:

At 45 minutes past two the signal was made for "closer action." The Niagara *being very little injured, I determined to pass through the Enemy's line; bore up, and passed ahead of their two Ships and a Brig, giving a raking fire to them from the Starboard guns, and to a large Schooner and Sloop from the Larboard side, at half Pistol shot distance.*

The British view agrees completely, according to Commander R.H. Barclay:

[T]he American Commodore seeing that as yet the day was against him… and also the very defenseless state of the Detroit, *which ship was now a perfect Wreck, principally from the Raking Fire of the Gunboats…made a noble, and alas, too successful an effort to regain it, for he bore up and supported by his small Vessels passed within Pistol Shot and took a raking position on our Bow, nor could I prevent it, as the unfortunate situation of the* Queen Charlotte *prevented us from wearing, in attempting it we fell onboard of her. My Gallant first Lieut. Garland was now mortally wounded and myself so severely that I was obliged to quit the deck.*

Barclay's account is worth close examination. He stated that the *Detroit* was now a wreck, understandably enough, but credited the major damage to the raking fire of the gunboats. Which ones? Certainly the *Scorpion* and *Ariel*, which had kept station on his weather bow throughout the action. Why not credit the *Lawrence* for more of his damage? Perhaps because so many of its guns were out of action early on, the *Detroit* received less fire from it. It's more likely that fire from the *Lawrence* was on the broadside, while the raking fire of the gunboats *Ariel* and *Scorpion* was proportionately worse, as the shot traveled the length of his deck. Barclay agreed with Perry on the extremely short range and described a catastrophic maneuver that resulted in a collision between the *Queen Charlotte* and the *Detroit*.

By this time, Barclay had received his second wound and was below deck, so his report was based on the previously mentioned report of Second Lieutenant Inglis. When we last left Inglis, the *Niagara* was moving into position to rake the *Detroit*: "[T]o prevent which in attempting to wear… fell onboard of the *Queen Charlotte*…as soon as we got clear of her I ordered the *Queen Charlotte* to shoot ahead of us if possible…but that ship laying completely unmanageable, every brace cut away…not a Stay left forward, Hull shattered very much."

The words "fell onboard" indicate that the *Detroit* was backing down on, as much as being run into by, the *Queen Charlotte*. Wearing ship, the process of turning a square-rigger to the opposite tack by making a downwind turn, would take more time and sea room than Barclay had at that moment. His damaged ships were not moving very fast and may have even still had the mainyards aback from being hove-to earlier. The way to increase the rate of turn in this situation is to point the main and mizzen yards into the wind (feathered position to minimize resistance) and back the foreyards (to push its head away from the wind). This maneuver proved impossible due to the amount of rigging that had been shot away. In any case, in addition to pushing its bow downwind, the likely effect of backing the foreyards on a slowly moving vessel would be to make a sternboard (back up).

The extensive damage to *Queen Charlotte*'s rigging precluded any evasive action, so with the wind shoving it forward and the *Detroit* both backing down and swinging across its course, the *Queen Charlotte* rammed its bowsprit through the *Detroit*'s starboard mizzen shrouds. The two vessels were locked together and helpless to maneuver. This British catastrophe allowed Perry to rake both ships with the same broadside. Some authors have attributed this collision to casualties among senior officers that left junior officers of limited experience in charge of both ships. The American fire had taken a heavy toll throughout the British squadron, according to Barclay: "And never in any Action was the loss more severe, every Officer Commanding Vessels and their Seconds was either killed, or Wounded so severely as to be unable to keep the deck."

On board the *Queen Charlotte*, with Captain Finnis dead and Lieutenant Stokoe wounded, inexperienced Provincial Marine lieutenant Irvine was left in command. It is possible that had he a better situational awareness and anticipated the *Detroit*'s response to Perry's maneuver, he might have avoided the collision. Situational awareness, however, is much easier to write about from a desk than maintain amid deafening cannons, choking smoke and bleeding men. It probably made no difference what Irvine understood or ordered—with so much of its essential rigging shot away, the *Queen Charlotte* was out of control.

With their leadership struck down, heavy casualties in the ranks, ships badly damaged and unmaneuverable and Americans guns at "can't miss" range, the British position became hopeless. Perry had the wind aft as he crossed their bows. As *Niagara* slid past, only a few feet from the end of the *Detroit*'s jibboom, its sails crossed the afternoon sun and threw a shadow of doom over the *Detroit*. *Niagara*'s guns had been double-shotted, a round of grapeshot atop each ball. As the guns came to bear, its starboard broadside was fired in rapid succession. In the space of perhaps six seconds, more than six hundred pounds of hot metal came scything down the length of the British ships in a great blast of fire and smoke. The greatest part of the British casualties likely came from this particular point-blank broadside.

Simultaneously, the *Niagara*'s larboard (port) broadside swept the decks of the schooner *Lady Prevost*, which had sailed around the two locked British ships only to be raked across its stern. The *Lady Prevost* was a converted merchant vessel with thin, low bulwarks and only twelve-pounder carronades. When its crew beheld *Niagara* bearing down on it, with a row of thirty-two-pounders run out, the men very understandably felt stark naked and defenseless. Just in time, they broke from their stations and dove headlong down the hatches. As the *Niagara*'s broadside tore through the ship, the only casualty was its commander, RN lieutenant Edward Buchan, who stayed on deck shouting for his men to stand to their guns and do their duty. Surprisingly, Buchan survived, albeit with his face smashed in by a grapeshot ball.

The instant the *Niagara* had loosed both broadsides, Perry ordered the helm hard down and rounded up to starboard, throwing the yards aback to stop abeam and to leeward of the ships he had just raked. In the time it took to man the braces and reload the starboard guns, the British survivors had chopped away enough rigging to let the *Queen Charlotte* separate from the *Detroit*, but to no avail. Seconds later, another broadside from the *Niagara* crashed through the bulwarks of both British ships.

At nearly the same moment, the small British brig *Hunter* had the misfortune to come out of the smoke just to leeward (downwind) of the *Niagara*'s lee bow. *Niagara*'s larboard (port/left side) guns had not been reloaded, but its marines rushed to the bulwarks and swept the *Hunter*'s deck with a massed volley of musketry. Moments later, the *Detroit* and the *Queen Charlotte* surrendered. Taylor's log entry states that the major British vessels had surrendered by 2:50 p.m. The *Chippewa* and the *Little Belt*, at the ends of the British line, made a run for Amherstburg. They were soon overtaken by the *Scorpion* and *Trippe*. The splash of a few balls close astern was enough to compel their surrender. Stephen Champlin of the *Scorpion* claimed to have fired the first and last American shots of the battle. By 3:15 p.m., all firing had ceased.

As the afternoon breeze cleared the smoke, the ships of both sides were intermingled. Many of the vessels could no longer maneuver, and the wind was carrying them farther away from Put-in-Bay. The longer they remained underway, the more scattered they would become. Within a few minutes, all had anchored. Sending an officer and prize crew on board each of

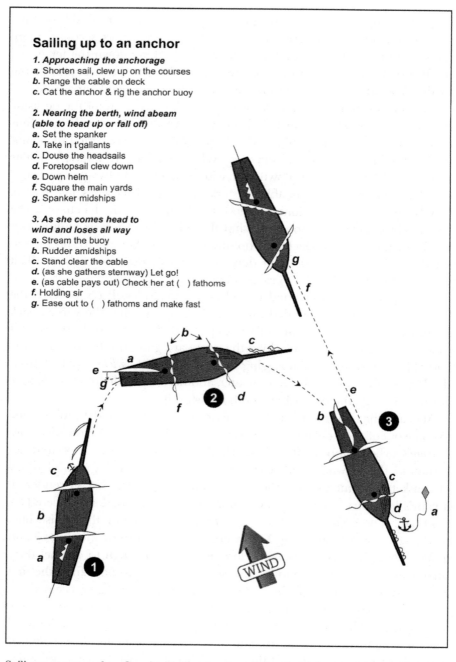

Sailing up to an anchor

1. Approaching the anchorage
a. Shorten sail, clew up on the courses
b. Range the cable on deck
c. Cat the anchor & rig the anchor buoy

**2. Nearing the berth, wind abeam
(able to head up or fall off)**
a. Set the spanker
b. Take in t'gallants
c. Douse the headsails
d. Foretopsail clew down
e. Down helm
f. Square the main yards
g. Spanker midships

**3. As she comes head to
wind and loses all way**
a. Stream the buoy
b. Rudder amidships
c. Stand clear the cable
d. (as she gathers sternway) Let go!
e. (as cable pays out) Check her at (   ) fathoms
f. Holding sir
g. Ease out to (   ) fathoms and make fast

Sailing up to an anchor. Care had to be taken in stopping badly damaged ships. Fortunately, the weather immediately after the battle allowed anchoring in the open lake.

the British vessels was a priority. The most immediate tasks were securing prisoners, aiding the wounded and making emergency repairs to the ships. Many of the ship's boats had been smashed to splinters. It was over an hour before a boat was available to return Perry to the *Lawrence*.

Once the immediate orders had been given to anchor and secure the captured ships, their execution and further details were up to subordinates. Perry would have suddenly been alone with his thoughts. As the completeness of the victory and the enormity of its consequences sunk in, he lost no time in reporting in two short messages. The first and best known was to General William H. Harrison, according to Perry: "We have met the enemy and they are ours; Two Ships, two Brigs, one Schooner & one Sloop. Yours with great respect and esteem."

The original of the message to Harrison does not survive. It has variously been described as written in pencil or ink on the back of an envelope. At the time, letters were commonly folded on themselves and sealed with wax, so it is probably more correct to state that the message was written on the back of an old letter. A more memorable report has never been written.

The second report, to Secretary of the Navy Jones, was more formal:

U.S. Brig Niagara off The Western Sister, Head of Lake Erie
Sepr. 10th, 1813   4 p.m.

Sir,

It has pleased the Almighty to give to the arms of the United States a signal victory over their enemies on this Lake—The British squadron consisting of two Ships, two Brigs, one Schooner & one Sloop have this moment surrendered to the force under my command, after a Sharp conflict.

I have the honor to be Sir Very Respectfully Your Obdt. Srvt.
O.H. Perry

Perry returned to the *Lawrence* for an emotional reunion with the survivors of his own crew. He wanted them to have the satisfaction of witnessing the formal surrender of the British officers, those who were still capable of getting into a boat and offering their swords in person. As was the custom to acknowledge a gallant foe, Perry allowed all to keep their personal arms.

AFTERMATH AND
CONSEQUENCES

Lake Erie, late afternoon, September 10, 1813.

After three hours of heavy firing in hot, still air, amid choking clouds of black powder smoke, the victors were nearly as dazed as the vanquished. Exhausted, throats parched and ears ringing, all picked their way over splintered decks slippery with gore, dismembered bodies and dismounted guns. The most prominent sound as their hearing slowly returned was the anguish of more than one hundred wounded, lying without anesthetics within the small clustered anchorage. On board the American vessels, dead seamen were sewn into their hammocks, weighted with shot and buried in the lake the night of the battle. Land being so near, the dead officers of both sides were held on board for shore burial.

Damage control parties worked through the night to secure tottering masts and plug shot holes near the waterline. The British prisoners outnumbered the Americans, who feared a prisoner revolt. For men who were hungry, exhausted and defeated, hand-to-hand combat in the dark was likely the last thing on their minds. Yet one can't fault the Americans for being careful. The surviving boats were kept busy rowing between the anchored vessels redistributing the British crews in smaller lots. A number of prisoners were ferried over to the *Lawrence* and confined to the berth deck, while all of the American wounded were brought up from the berth deck to the fresh air of the weather deck. Sailing Master Taylor worked far into the night jury-rigging repairs to the shattered rig of the *Lawrence*. In a letter to his wife, he described Perry sleeping atop an arms chest, his own arms folded across his breast, clutching the hilt of his sword in one hand and a pistol in the other in case the prisoners rose.

The ships that had been in the thick of the battle were a gory shambles. Elliott had gone on board the *Detroit* to take possession of it. He slipped in a puddle of blood and fell onto the deck, so soaking his white uniform pants that when he reported to Perry that evening, his commander's first words were, "Are you wounded?" For those who were wounded, treatment was a long time coming. The surgeons were debilitated with lake fever. The task of caring for most of the seriously wounded of both sides fell on surgeon's mate Usher Parsons. He treated more than one hundred wounded and lost only four, better than a 96 percent survival rate. Such success was unheard of at the time and not bettered until World War I (and even then only in select areas).

Parsons took some measures that were highly beneficial, even if not understood at the time. During the battle, the rate at which the wounded were coming down overwhelmed him. He only had time to stop bleeding and splint shattered limbs, amputating only those hanging on by a strip of flesh. The night after the battle, rather than perform surgery by candlelight, Parsons elected to wait on all operations until the next morning, when he performed surgeries on deck in the bright daylight versus the usual practice of surgery by dim candle light below decks during a battle. Also, by the next morning, his patients had recovered somewhat from the exhaustion and dehydration of the battle. Parsons also made a practice of keeping his instruments in a bucket of hot water, reasoning that his patients would feel less pain if the surgeon's instruments were at approximate body temperature. Although short of sterilization, the instruments were at least rinsed. Taken together, these factors, combined with Parsons's dedication, yielded a surprisingly high survival rate.

While Parsons amputated and stitched that morning, the breeze was gentle out of the southwest. The now combined squadrons got underway at 0900 and by noon were anchored in Put-in-Bay. That night, a storm was building, and by 0500 Sunday, it was blowing a gale. The badly damaged *Queen Charlotte* dragged anchor and fouled the *Detroit* again. As their yards locked, both ships were completely dismasted. This storm was a further example of Perry's phenomenal luck. Had the wind remained at southeast after the battle, he could not have sailed back to the shelter of Put-in-Bay. Had he been caught in open water by this gale, it is very likely that the more heavily damaged vessels would have sunk, with great loss of life. Later that morning, the gale died down, and a procession of boats carried the dead officers of both sides ashore on South Bass Island, where they were buried together after a service attended by the surviving officers of both squadrons.

By the evening of September 12, 1813, following the officers' funeral, Perry transferred his flag to the U.S. schooner *Ariel*, and his correspondence was headed from this vessel for the rest of the campaign. Apparently, Perry did not wish to displace Elliott from the *Niagara* nor share a ship with his presence. On a very practical level, there were no enemy ships left to fight, and the two large brigs were now a liability in terms of draft and lack of windward ability. What Perry needed was rapid communication between himself and General Harrison, which the *Ariel* provided since it was the fastest vessel on the lake.

The *Lawrence* was a shattered wreck. A visitor coming on board when the squadron reached Put-in-Bay the day after the battle described the ship as "not a hand's breadth of unblemished wood could be found between splintered planks, decks clotted with blood, and bits of hair, teeth, and bone imbedded in the bulwarks." The *Lawrence* had also become the hospital ship and, under the command of Lieutenant Yarnall, weighed anchor on September 21, bound for Erie with all of the seriously wounded. Three days later, on the twenty-third, the *Lawrence* came to anchor off Erie, and the wounded were lightered off to quarters in the town.

Back at the western end of the lake, now that the Americans had established total naval superiority, the British had no hope of adequate resupply, and their position became untenable. For the Americans, the days following the battle went into transporting Harrison's small army from Sandusky, Ohio, to the Canadian shore. About three thousand men and several hundred horses were landed. The move was accomplished primarily in a fleet of seventy-five bateaux that had been built in Cleveland earlier that summer. Leapfrogging from island to island, the movement took seven days from September 20, culminating in a landing at Bar Point, just east of the Detroit River on the twenty-seventh.

The American squadron took on some of the troops, but the primary mission was to supply artillery support for the landing, if needed. It wasn't needed. By the time they arrived, the British had abandoned their positions and burned Fort Malden. The British retreated up the Detroit River, along the shore of Lake St. Clair and then up the Thames River, heading east into Ontario. Harrison, after regarrisoning Fort Detroit, pursued the retreating British column. Perry sailed the lightest-draft vessels—*Porcupine, Tigress* and *Somers*—up the Detroit River and across Lake St Clair to the Thames River, and then upriver alongside Harrison's line of march, to provide artillery support should it be needed. Eventually, the banks on either side rose higher than the guns could be elevated. Not only were the gunboats no longer of any offensive use, but they also became vulnerable to having their decks swept by small arms fire should the British or Indians attack. Perry ordered them to drop back to a safer position.

With the British in headlong retreat on October 2, Perry delegated temporary command of the squadron to Elliott and volunteered as aide-de-camp to General Harrison. This was another of Perry's typically rash moves. Even though the British naval force had been completely defeated, Perry was still responsible for the safety of his squadron against threats of weather and navigational hazards. He also had responsibility for the scores of wounded men, hundreds of prisoners, badly damaged ships facing possible Indian attack and worsening fall weather, not to mention the possibility that at any moment orders might arrive from either Chauncey or the secretary of the navy to send the squadron to the Niagara River area or transfer personnel to Lake Ontario. Yet Perry blithely turned all of this over to Elliott to mount a horse and essentially become a tourist riding alongside Harrison for the rest of the land campaign.

The end of the campaign, however, was near. Outside Moraviantown (near present-day London, Ontario) on October 5, the overtaken British and Indian force attempted to make a stand. The British had not formed a compact line when U.S. mounted volunteers charged through their ranks, which quickly dissolved into a rout. The Indians dispersed into the woods, save a few score closest and most loyal to Tecumseh who stood firm with him and resolved to fight to the death. The Kentuckians made certain this was so. Shouting "Remember the Raisin" and bent on revenge, they persisted until there were no Indian prisoners. (The Battle of the River Raisin in January 1813, near Monroe, Michigan, was a U.S. defeat, after which scores of wounded prisoners were massacred by the Indians.) Despite the complete tactical victory, Harrison recognized that he was in danger of being overextended and lost no time making up his mind. The Americans were back to their vessels in Lake St. Clair by October 7.

It is tempting to speculate that an opportunity was lost to turn the British flank in Ontario, but Harrison's instincts were sound. Between his forces and the U.S. territory to the east lay 150 miles of enemy country. The extent of the defenses, if any, was not known, and the depth of further Indian resistance remained a wild card. Autumn rains were making the very bad road all but impassable (it was the absence of good roads that had made the lake so crucial). Having won a victory, shattering the opposing force,

Harrison chose to consolidate his gains. He fell back to Detroit, garrisoned it and Fort Malden with regulars and sent the time-expired militia home. Harrison requested transport for himself and as many of his regulars as could be carried to join the U.S. forces in Buffalo. The *Detroit* and *Queen Charlotte* were left in Put-in-Bay for the winter since there was no way to re-rig them in time and since the rest of the squadron sailed to Erie, arriving on November 2. Here Perry gave his final orders before signing over command of the squadron to Elliott. On November 5, Perry and Harrison sailed to Buffalo, arriving the next day.

Perry had written to the secretary of the navy requesting leave and a transfer off the lakes. Perry's victory was too much of an event to let slip without making the most out of it for revival of national morale. The ride home took three weeks, with nearly every town along the way offering banquets, testimonials and gifts. By November 28, Perry was home in Newport.

The squadron that he left in Erie lay clustered to moorings in Little Bay, on the peninsula. Roofs of bark were improvised over them, and a blockhouse/hospital was built ashore. The winter was harsh and morale plummeted. So many died of illness that the anchorage was renamed Misery Bay, the name it still bears. To add to the physical hardships, numerous quarrels surfaced among the officers, two of whom were killed in duels. Elliott felt insulted to be given a command with no enemy to fight. Eventually, Chauncey sent his flag captain, Arthur Sinclair, to relieve Elliott, who then returned to Lake Ontario as commanding officer of the twenty-gun brig *Jefferson*, serving under Chauncey for the remainder of 1814. Sinclair described the Erie squadron as being in deplorable condition, with repairs incomplete, morale and discipline in tatters and accounts a mess. Sinclair did eventually get the squadron in shape to sail in 1814.

The assessment of the Battle of Lake Erie as a turning point in the war is overrated. For both sides, Detroit was at the extreme western end of a long supply line. Neither side had the strength or resources to turn the other's flank. If Barclay had defeated Perry, the British would not have been able to mount any further attempts at invading Ohio. As it was, even with complete naval supremacy on Lake Erie and a British military collapse, Harrison could do no more than occupy vacated positions. Rolling up the British flank along the Niagara front was simply too large a task for a force with such small resources. Despite Perry's victory and the retaking of Detroit, the year 1813 did not end well for the United States. The Niagara Peninsula had been retaken by the British, who then crossed the Niagara River to burn the towns of Black Rock and Buffalo. Fort Niagara was captured in a

Battle of the Thames, October 5, 1813. Loss of their naval squadron forced the British to abandon Detroit and Amherstburg and enabled General Harrison to land unopposed and pursue the retreating British/Indian force. The Shawnee chief Tecumseh is killed, leading to collapse of the Indian-British alliance. *Battle of the Thames and the Death of Tecumseh, by the Kentucky Mounted Volunteers led by Genl. Macomb, Sept 17th 1814*, painted by H. Reinagle, engraved by B. Tanner. *Courtesy Library of Congress.*

nighttime raid in December 1813 and remained in British hands to the end of the war.

By March 1814, with Napoleon defeated and in exile, the British could shift resources to the American war, with dire consequences to the United States. It was clear that despite the growing competence of the U.S. Army, the country was in serious danger of being militarily overwhelmed. In September 1814, the United States sought to negotiate a peace. Commissioners from both sides met in Ghent, Belgium, to begin a protracted process. The British, though eager to be done with the conflict, felt that they had the upper hand and initially sought significant concessions, such as possession of forts on both shores of the Great Lakes. Their primary aim was to make it much more difficult for the United States to launch future invasions of Canada. The American negotiating team was adamant against such concessions and, sensing the British weariness, chose to wait them out.

In the defense of Baltimore in the Chesapeake campaign, and in halting the invasion of New York at Plattsburgh Bay, the Americans narrowly escaped disaster. For the British, these failures made clear that to accomplish anything decisive would require a much greater level of effort. The government turned to the Duke of Wellington, its most successful general, and offered him command in North America. Wellington felt duty bound to accept but saw no prospect of success and instead offered blunt advice on November 9, 1814, according to Mahan's *Seapower*:

> *If the government wanted conquests in North America, what was needed was not a general, or general officers and troops, but naval superiority on the Lakes. Till that superiority is acquired, it is impossible, according to my notion, to maintain an army in such a situation as to keep the enemy out of the whole frontier, much less to make any conquest from the enemy...The question is whether we can obtain this naval superiority on the lakes. If we cannot, I shall do you but little good in America; and I shall go there only to prove the truth of Prevost's defense, and to sign a peace which might as well be signed now.*

The lead British negotiator later commented that "if we had burned Baltimore or taken Plattsburgh we may have been able to press on." The British abandoned their demands, and in turn the Americans dropped the issue of impressment. Both sides eventually agreed to end the war at the antebellum status quo. In large measure, this was possible because the territory controlled by both sides was virtually the same as it had been in 1812. It is only here at the end of the war that the true strategic significance of the Battle of Lake Erie becomes apparent. If the battle had not been fought or had been a draw, or if Perry had been defeated, the British would likely have retained their hold on Detroit. More importantly, the alliance with Tecumseh's Indian confederacy might have remained intact.

The British would then have been in a strong position to demand acceptance of the borders based on the military situation. As a result, the U.S.-Canadian border might today run along the Ohio-Michigan line. The consequence of Michigan remaining Indian country under British protection would have greatly encouraged Native American resistance to further U.S. expansion. A future war would have been very likely. Perry's victory, by enabling the United States to regain territory bungled away at the outset of the war, broke the British-Indian alliance and restored the prewar strategic balance. The twin naval victories of Lake Erie and Lake Champlain, more than any other battles, allowed the nation to emerge intact from the war.

THE PERRY-ELLIOTT
CONTROVERSY

In the nearly two centuries since the Battle of Lake Erie was fought, at least as much ink has been expended on the ensuing acrimony between Perry and Elliott as on the battle itself. Perry's after-action report, written two days after the battle, states that "Captain Elliott behaved with his customary gallantry." This sounds guarded but was not as tepid as it sounds. Recall that Elliott had been awarded a medal and a sword by Congress for the daring cutting-out expedition to capture two vessels from under the guns of Fort Erie the preceding fall. After Perry sent his report, he became aware of how much resentment was felt toward Elliott within the squadron, especially by the officers and men of the *Lawrence*. Perry ordered that there be no show of dissension. A great victory had been won, and there was no need to mar it with bickering.

But it was too late, and probably an impossible expectation regardless. Immediately after the battle, some of the *Lawrence*'s officers wrote letters home describing the battle and airing complaints against Elliott. Some letters found their way to being quoted or reproduced in newspapers. Elliott soon got wind of this and demanded additional support from Perry. By then, Perry had had some time to think about it and refused to embellish his original account or to write anything else to vindicate Elliott.

Why was Perry so vague and circumspect in his initial report to the secretary of the navy? Perhaps he was feeling "survivor guilt" for having impetuously led his men on board the *Lawrence* into a slaughter while a great part of his own fleet's strength lay just out of range. The realization may have sunk in for Perry that in his haste to prove himself, he had greatly increased the deadliness of the situation and survived it only by the merest chance. At the same time, it couldn't have escaped Elliott that despite his qualms and correct analysis of Perry's rash risk-taking, the breeze did hold long enough to get into close action, and he had failed to support his commander then, and later, through making no attempt to close the range for the next two murderous hours. Salting his raw conscience was the plain fact that the rest of the squadron knew it. If not cowardice, Elliott's conduct was at least insubordination and extreme stubbornness, but the former is the charge he most feared from his peers.

By that time, Elliott was distraught enough to seek a stronger statement of approval from Perry. He probably reasoned that it was unlikely that Perry would contradict his already submitted report. Elliott's timing was off. Perry had by then realized that while his own leadership had been less than tactically brilliant, he had been let down and nearly betrayed by Elliott. Therefore, Perry refused to alter a word or write another report. Adding to Elliott's anguish must have been the feeling that he had been robbed of vindication by Perry's boat transfer to the *Niagara*. When the wind filled in that afternoon, not only was the *Niagara* driven forward, but the dense clouds of powder smoke were also blown to leeward, clearing the visibility. Elliott grasped the shattered state of the *Lawrence*, as well as the severe damage to the *Detroit* and *Queen Charlotte*. He understood that he had the chance to redeem the situation and close in with a fresh ship, turning defeat into victory. Just at his moment of triumph, Elliott sees Perry, who by Elliott's judgment had wretchedly mismanaged the battle, climbing on board to snatch fame and glory out of the opportunity Elliott was in process of seizing.

Evidence that Elliott felt robbed is seen in his embracing the British version of the timing of Lieutenant Yarnall's striking the ensign on board the *Lawrence*. American accounts are nearly unanimous in claiming that Yarnall waited until Perry was on board *Niagara* before striking. Both British and Canadian accounts are nearly unanimous that the flag came down immediately after Perry departed. The dispute hinges on interpretation of a point of honor. In single-ship actions, striking the ensign clearly signaled surrender. In a fleet action, it was an open question whether the loss of the flagship obliged the others to surrender as well. The implication is that Perry's resuming the fight after his flagship had struck was not quite honorable.

This is overreaching. Whatever the timing, Barclay had no illusion that Perry had surrendered. His own after-action report mentions Perry's transfer as "intended to regain the day." Besides, it is rather un-British to blaze away at men in a small boat fleeing a beaten ship that has already surrendered, isn't it? The *Detroit's* officers knew very well that the fight was not over. Yet a few weeks later, according to a letter to Perry from Purser Hambleton, during the time Perry rode with General Harrison and left Elliott in temporary command of the squadron, a discussion had taken place among the officers concerning their likely prize money. Elliott let slip that since the *Lawrence* had surrendered before the end of the battle, none of its men would be eligible for prize money. In fact, he argued that as a recaptured ship, the value of the *Lawrence* should be added on the British side to increase the shares for all the other Americans. As acting squadron commander, Elliott could make such an outrageous assertion without risk of challenge from subordinates. But to be so crass and to have the gall to discount the sacrifice and courage of the *Lawrence*'s crew in front of fellow officers reveals the depth of bitterness gnawing at Elliott.

Despite the ill will of the squadron, Elliott fared well in Washington, where he was already known as a decorated veteran. Lake Erie is the only battle of the War of 1812 in which the second in command received the same gold medal as the commander and, initially, the same prize money (although subsequently Perry was awarded an additional bonus). As the war went on and attention shifted to new events, criticism of Elliott faded, and he appeared to have weathered the storm. It was particularly galling to Elliott to recognize that his good standing was largely due to Perry's forbearance. Each soon came to regard the other as an ungrateful wretch. Elliott convinced himself that Perry owed the victory to Elliott's actions and was denying him the recognition he deserved. Perry regretted ever having "shielded" Elliott and grew more contemptuous of him.

A little over a year after the battle, the transcript of Commander R.H. Barclay's court-martial in England was released, published and found its way to American readers. Barclay was honorably acquitted for fighting bravely against a stronger squadron. Within the testimony is an assertion by the *Queen Charlotte*'s officers that they had closed up with the *Detroit* against the *Lawrence* because the *Niagara* had stayed out of range. This rekindled the dispute, and Elliott asked the navy for an inquiry to clear his name. The inquiry was convened in New York in February 1815. Few witnesses were called other than Elliott's junior officers from the *Niagara*. These young officers' professional advancement was largely influenced by the recommendation that Elliott would make when they came up for promotion. Perry was not called to testify, although he was only two days away at his home in Newport.

The navy's interest was to counter any ill reflection on the honor of the navy, not to find out exactly what happened. The questions were what today's journalistic parlance would call "softballs." Elliott was asked, "Were you continuously engaged?" to which he could answer yes because his twelve-pounder long guns fired at extreme range every few minutes throughout the battle. "Were you at any time making way to get away from the battle?" This was of course denied.

At no point was Elliott asked, "Did you do your utmost to closely engage and support your commander?" The navy duly ruled that no dishonor to the service had occurred. One would think that Elliott would now leave well enough alone.

Not so. Elliott's wounded psyche continued to seek greater recognition for winning the battle, and correspondence among officers who had served at Lake Erie became partisan and shrill. When asked by his supporters why he would not come out and condemn Elliott, Perry replied, "It is better to shield a coward in our ranks than to let the enemy know we have one." Although the war ended, the innuendo carried on for years. Eventually, Elliott challenged Perry to a duel. Perry declined, giving Elliott the opportunity to silence him, but stipulated that if Elliott would submit to stand trial before a court-martial and be exonerated, then Perry would meet him in a duel if he still desired. This reply chilled Elliott's ardor for a duel but incensed Perry, who fixated on pressing charges against Elliott.

The secretary of the navy wanted no such thing. Having two decorated veterans and senior officers washing dirty linen in public over past events would not reflect well on the navy, whatever the outcome. As a practical matter, convening a fair trial would be problematic, since many witnesses were by now deceased and others were at sea on distant stations. The secretary solved the problem by offering Perry a seagoing command as commodore of a squadron carrying the ambassador to newly independent Venezuela. Seagoing commands were limited in the peacetime navy. Perry promptly accepted and sailed away. The secretary may well have been thinking to get Perry out of the country before a duel was provoked. The offer may have been contingent upon a verbal agreement that Perry drop the idea of pressing charges against Elliott. Perry never returned from this mission. He died of yellow fever on his thirty-fourth birthday, on August 23, 1819, anchored in the Orinoco River. Elliott never received vindication, but with Perry gone, the issue was likely to fade away. That is, until Elliott brought it to the fore again through his own ineptitude in another affair.

In March 1820, the nation was shocked and saddened to learn that Captain Stephan Decatur, its most famous naval hero, had died as a result of a duel with Captain James Barron, a fellow officer who had lived under a cloud since the ignominy and humiliation of the U.S. frigate *Chesapeake*'s being fired upon by HMS *Leopard* in 1807. The circumstances of this particular case are a long story best told elsewhere. Of significance here, however, is that Elliott served as Barron's second in this sordid business. The role of seconds in a duel was to make the physical arrangements to ensure that the combat was as equal as possible—swords the same length, pistols matched and loaded properly and so on. But the most important part of the role was to seek reconciliation if at all possible so that the challenge could be cancelled.

By this time, the point of a duel was for the participants to prove their courage by accepting the risk of death or maiming. Most duels ended after both antagonists fired a single shot and missed. In this absurd ritual, both Elliott and Bainbridge thoroughly disgraced themselves. They agreed to a less-than-standard range, increasing the chance of a lethal hit, and made no attempt at dissuading their principals. Even as they met on the field, Barron said to Decatur, "Sir, I have never been your enemy," to which Decatur replied, "Nor I yours." Either statement should have been all the prompting needed for both seconds to step in and announce that there had obviously been a misunderstanding, that both duelists had proved their courage by showing up and standing pistol in hand and that everyone should now go home. No such intervention occurred. What poisonous mix of resentment, envy or anger drove Elliott and Bainbridge? It is doubtful that we will ever know. Both duelists were hit. Barron suffered a recoverable wound, and Decatur was hit in the lower abdomen, condemning him to long hours of agony before an early, futile, useless death.

Before Perry had sailed away the previous year, he had left a copy of his charges against Elliott with his friend Decatur. Most likely, the intent was to have some defense in place should Elliott come forth with accusations of his own in Perry's absence. Decatur's widow, both aggrieved and enraged at the almost engineered death of her husband, rightly regarded the seconds as accessories to murder. In going through Decatur's desk afterward, she came upon Perry's charges against Elliott. These she took to a printer and had four hundred copies printed and hardbound, for distribution around Washington. As embarrassing as this was for Elliott, with Perry dead, it had nowhere to go and again faded out.

Years later, in 1838, James Fenimore Cooper published a history of the U.S. Navy in which he sought to magnify U.S. accomplishments by praising everyone, including both Perry and Elliott. Shortly thereafter, in 1842, Messieurs Burges, Duer and Mackenzie published their opinion of the battle that was far more critical of Elliott and that Cooper felt compelled to rebut in 1843. By now, it was seen as an academic argument. Elliott went on to a long career in the navy, demonstrating on several occasions a knack for enraging people but nevertheless surviving to die still in uniform as commandant of the Philadelphia Navy Yard in 1845, at which time he was fifty-three years old. The navy has never named a ship for Jesse Duncan Elliott. Seven have borne the name of Perry. The "Don't Give Up the Ship" flag is prominently displayed at the Naval Academy in Annapolis.

THE *NIAGARA* LIVES ON

RECONSTRUCTIONS OF THE *NIAGARA*

The original *Niagara*, as well as its sister ship the *Lawrence*, last sailed in 1814. The navy maintained a minimal presence at the Erie naval station until 1820. When the station was disbanded, the large brigs were reported both as being beached and sunk. The records are spotty and contradictory. The smaller vessels were sold off for merchant service after the war. What was believed to be the *Lawrence* was sent to Philadelphia for the centennial exposition in 1876, where the exhibit hall and the remains of the vessel were lost to a fire. The local knowledge believed the remaining hull to be the *Niagara*, and this has been accepted by PHMC. There is no way of knowing for sure, but does it matter? The two were sister ships, built together and fought together. The story of the Lake Erie squadron remains the same whichever vessel's remains were raised.

THE RECONSTRUCTION OF 1913

In 1913, for the 100th anniversary of the Battle of Lake Erie, the remains of the original *Niagara* were brought up from the bottom of Misery Bay. The intent was to rebuild the wreck into a floating exhibit in time for commemorative events. What remained was the ship's bottom out to the turn of the bilge on the starboard side, the stem and stern posts and on the port side nearly half the midship length carried up through the bulwarks. Original information learned from the wreck was embodied in the 1913 vessel and in subsequent

For the centennial of the Battle of Lake Erie in 1913, the reconstructed brig *Niagara* was towed around the lakes by the *Wolverine*. Commissioned in 1844 as *Michigan*, this ship was the USN's longest-serving steamship. In 1905, it was transferred to the Pennsylvania Naval Militia, a precursor of the Navy Reserves, and steamed a few weeks each summer on training cruises. *Courtesy the Bolla family.*

"rebuildings," "restorations" and "reconstructions." The length and size of keel, rake of stem and stern posts, degree of deadrise, depth of hold, spacing of deck beams and dimensions of planking and framing were all evident, as was the size and spacing of the iron fastenings. The remains of mast steps on the keelson gave the spacing but not the rake of the masts. The size and spacing of gun ports, as well as the sweep ports and the method of securing gun tackle (with forelock keys), could all be established.

A number of pieces of frame and floor futtocks were retained and not used in the reconstruction. These pieces are still in the possession of the PHMC. The commemorative *Niagara* was towed on a tour of the Great Lakes by the *Wolverine* from July to September 1913. Ports visited were Fairport, Lorain, Put-in-Bay, Monroe, Toledo, Milwaukee, Green Bay, Chicago, Buffalo, Sandusky and Detroit.

After this tour was over, no one had any idea what to do with the *Niagara*. This second vessel had a very similar history to the original. It was built hurriedly, again with a great deal of green wood, to meet a short-term need. After the immediate need passed, the ship again became a liability for its owners. *Niagara* was berthed in Erie, initially as a tourist attraction, and proceeded to rot away. Beginning in 1933, funds were raised for intermittent work on another rebuild. A few hands and a trickle of money found the hull ready to launch by October 1943. By coincidence, on launching day, October 5, it stuck on the ways just as the original had in 1813. In November 1943, the hull was towed across the bay to the West Canal Basin and remained afloat until the land could be purchased and a dry-berth cradle built. This took until early 1945, by which time the present-day PHMC had been chartered to replace the Pennsylvania Historical Commission. This third incarnation of *Niagara* sat on this cradle from 1945 to 1988.

THE PRESENT *NIAGARA* (1988–)

By the 1970s, it was becoming obvious that although dry-berthing a ship eliminated the threat of its sinking, destruction through decay was still an issue. PHMC had long recognized that the ship sitting on a concrete cradle and with next to no maintenance was slowly turning into last year's pumpkin. By 1986, PHMC had received an initial appropriation of $1million and was able to put out a Request for Proposal for research and design for a restoration of the brig. The design contract was awarded to Melbourne Smith, International Historic Watercraft Society, who subsequently received the construction contract as well.

Smith conducted his own research, including study of surviving drawings of other vessels built by Noah Brown. To assemble the craftsmen and run the construction project, Melbourne subcontracted Bill Elliott of Bay Ship and Yacht from Sausalito, California. The hull was completed in the very quick time of ninety days. A crew of about twenty-five was employed on site, and full advantage was taken of every modern power tool.

Once again, a commemorative event, the 175th anniversary of the Battle of Lake Erie, pushed the schedule. The largest crowd in Erie's living memory lined the shores of Presque Isle Bay to see the launching on September 10, 1988. The hull was launched by a very large crane with much ceremony, but the empty shell next sat at its berth for more than a year, awaiting funding for completion of the interior and the entirety of the rig. Finally, additional appropriations were found, and in the winter of 1990, Melbourne Smith and Bill Elliott returned to Erie to finish the ship, at least sufficient for a sea trial.

The preservation project that had begun with studies and surveys in the late '70s had taken more than ten years to arrive at a ship afloat, rigged and ready for a sail. Finally, on July 18, 1990, *Niagara* was towed out for a sea trial before acceptance by the PHMC. Designer and project manager Melbourne Smith was, of course, on hand. The builder, Bill Elliott, and his crew had done some dockside training, assigning crew members to specific lines. Melbourne Smith had engaged Captain Carl Bowman (USCG, retired), formerly captain of the *Eagle, Star of India* and *Elissa*, to be in command. It was a beautiful day with a good breeze, a proud day for the people of Erie and a joyous occasion as the culmination of a long effort. It was also a bittersweet day because the building crew was about to disperse, and no one knew for certain if the ship would ever sail again.

DEVELOPING THE SAILING PROGRAM (1991–)

When PHMC decided to rebuild *Niagara* as a floating vessel, the idea of sailing it was not far behind. There were, however, some significant obstacles. PHMC management recognized that they lacked the in-house expertise to implement such a program. The system had no job descriptions for professional mariners and was very slow to respond to contingencies. Upper management was agreed on the goal, if not the methodology. Executive Director Dr. Brent Glass was highly supportive throughout his tenure. Michael Ripton bore the unofficial title of "instigator" for his role in moving the project into reality. Jack Leighow had direct responsibility for oversight and was exactly the right person to accomplish the difficult and the unusual. In addition to being a most fair and reasonable manager, Jack had a knowledge level we called "a black belt in bureaucracy," coupled with an attitude of "there has to be a way to make this happen somehow." The instrument for implementing what amounted to an experimental program was to be the Flagship Niagara League (FNL), a private nonprofit chartered as a support group for PHMC and the *Niagara*.

Dr. Robert Knieb was the president of the league at the time and was doing his own investigation into what it would take to manage an active sailing vessel. With the active support of Dr. William Garvey, then president of Mercyhurst College, the FNL brought to Erie as consultants several experienced ship captains and ship restoration professionals. This seminar

Niagara sails throughout the Great Lakes, offering through experiential education programs and insights into history, as well as preservation of part of our cultural heritage. *Photo by John Baker.*

in November 1990 resulted in a realistic budget and established the broad parameters of what to look for in a captain, the whole to be in a proposal to PHMC to grant the FNL a sum in six figures to be used to hire a crew capable of maintaining the ship and sailing it to some ports. The end result was a recruitment phone call to me, offering a ticket to fly into Erie and discuss the job, which I was offered and accepted.

That summer of 1991 will always be reminiscent of the summer of 1813—a small group of saltwater professionals appeared at the last minute to recruit and train local volunteers, working long hours on a need-it-yesterday basis, to be able to sail to the historic site of Put-in-Bay, Ohio. The key ingredient was the right professional crew to accomplish not only the work needed on board but also the skills transfer that had to be imparted to the green but eager volunteer crew.

In this I was extremely fortunate that Dan Moreland was available and willing to take the chief mate's position that summer. He brought with him three others who shared a background of voyaging on the brigantine *Romance* under Captain Arthur Kimberly, including Kimberly himself. The story of how the vast body of knowledge, skills and traditions that collectively constitute "seamanship" survived, at least the essential core of it, during the roughly half century from the end of commercial sail to the revival of interest in the educational value of sail in the last quarter century is a tale of a few willing apprentices finding the right mentors to pass it on. It is a tale akin to having a few flints, scraps of iron and just enough kindling to keep some embers aglow as the gift of fire was passed across an ice age. But that is another story for another book.

Appendix I

GUN DRILL PROCEDURE

CARRONADE DRILL (APPLIES TO LONG GUNS AS WELL)

Start with unloaded gun secured.

1. Cast loose the gun (cast off lashings, pull tompion and uncover or affix gun lock).
2. Run in the gun (shift side tackles to inboard ringbolt and haul in).
3. Search the bore (run a worm down the muzzle to ensure that the bore is empty).
4. Load the charge (insert flannel powder bag in muzzle).
5. Ram the charge (ram bag to breech).
6. Check the charge is home (insert vent prick to be sure bag is all the way in).
7. Cover the vent (prevent entry of sparks or water).
8. Load the shot and wad (insert ball followed by wad in muzzle).
9. Ram home the shot (ram ball and wad back to seat against powder bag).
10. Run out the gun (haul on side tackles to run gun out to firing position).
11. Remove side tackles (unhook from carriage to avoid hindrance of recoil).
12. Prick and prime (uncover vent, insert prick to puncture powder bag, insert priming quill and add priming powder to pan of flintlock).

13. Check elevation and train and adjust as needed, flintlock to full cock.
14. Stand clear (don't get flattened by your own gun's recoil).
15. Fire (pull lanyard on flintlock, slowmatch is backup).

In action, starting from a hot gun just fired.

1. First two steps above not needed—recoil will have brought gun in.
2. Worm the bore (extract smoldering remnants of powder bag).
3. Sponge the gun (wet sponge is run in and out, while leather thumbstall is pressed over vent to prevent fresh air reaching any embers; sponge should be snug fit, making this the single hardest piece of work).
4. Dry sponge (to prevent wetting powder bag—after several rounds, this step could be skipped as the gun would be hot enough to sizzle off any excess water).
5. Remaining steps same as above, resume with loading the charge (no. 4 above).
6. Repeat as needed until surrender obtained.

Appendix II

USN RANKS AND PAY IN 1812

Admiral	(none until 1862)
Captain	$168 per month
Master Commandant	$100
Lieutenant	$75
Sailing Master	$57
Surgeon's Mate	$47
Marine Sergeant	$17
Able Seaman	$12
Ordinary Seaman	$8

Appendix III

BRITISH AND AMERICAN
SQUADRON COMPARISON

USN Vessel	Commanding Officer	Crew
Lawrence	Oliver H. Perry	136
Niagara	Jesse Elliott	155
Caledonia	Daniel Turner	53
Ariel	John Packet	36
Somers	Thomas Almy	30
Scorpion	Stephen Champlin	55
Porcupine	George Senat	25
Tigress	Augustus Conklin	27
Trippe	Thomas Holdup	35
Totals		532

RN Vessel	Commanding Officer	Crew
Detroit	Robert Barclay	150
Queen Charlotte	Robert Finnis	126
Lady Prevost	Edward Buchan	86
Hunter	George Bignell	45
Little Belt	(unknown)	18
Chippewa	John Campbell	15
Totals		440*

Most sources give a total of 440, but research of Altoff and Skaggs documents 572. The most probable explanation is that the difference is a number of last-minute reinforcements from the army with no record of the vessel to which they were temporarily assigned.

COMPARISON OF FIREPOWER OF THE LAKE ERIE SQUADRONS

USN

VESSEL	LONG GUNS	CARRONADES
Scorpion	(1) 32-pdr	(1) 24-pdr
Ariel	(4) 12-pdr	
Lawrence	(2) 12-pdr	(18) 32-pdr
Caledonia	(2) 24-pdr	(1) 32-pdr
Niagara	(2) 12-pdr	(18) 32-pdr
Somers	(1) 24-pdr	(1) 32-pdr
Porcupine	(1) 32-pdr	
Trippe	(1) 24-pdr	
Tigress	(1) 32-pdr	

RN

VESSEL	LONG GUNS	CARRONADES
Little Belt	(1) 9-pdr and (2) 6-pdr	
Detroit	(2) 24-pdr and (1) 18-pdr	(1) 24-pdr
	(6) 12-pdr and (8) 9-pdr	(1) 18-pdr
Hunter	(2) 6-pdr; (4) 4-pdr and (2) 2-pdr	(2) 12-pdr
Queen Charlotte	(3) 12-pdr	(14) 24-pdr
Lady Prevost	(3) 9-pdr	(10) 12-pdr
Chippeava	(1) 9-pdr	

INDEX

INDEX

ABOUT THE AUTHOR

Photo by John Baker.

B orn in Brooklyn, New York, in 1950, frequent visits to the harbor seeded Walter Rybka's maritime interest. His parents took their four children to museums of all kinds, as well as to many national parks and historic sites, which encouraged an interest in history. His career has been divided between preservation of historic ships for museums and experiential education programs sailing historic vessel types. In command of the reconstructed U.S. brig *Niagara* since 1991, he resides in Erie, Pennsylvania. He is married and has one daughter, who is now ten. He has a USCG license as master, auxiliary sail, 1,600 tons, oceans.

Visit us at
www.historypress.net

CPSIA information can be obtained
at www.ICGtesting.com
Printed in the USA
LVOW03*0402041017
551105LV00015B/467/P